REINVENTED TO RISE II

Stories of Perseverance, Strength, and Courage

Visionary Author
Dr Alethia Tucker

Copyright©2023 by Dr. Alethia Tucker

All rights reserved. No part of this publication may be reproduced, stored in a retrieval system, or transmitted, in any form or by any means, electronic, mechanical, photocopying, recording, or otherwise, without the prior written permission of the publisher. Printed in the United States of America.

For permission requests, write to the publisher, addressed "Attention: Permissions Coordinator", at the address below.

info@ joleaseenterprises.com

ISBN: Paperback: 979-8-9873658-1-6
Hardback: 979-8-3914614-8-7

Ordering Information:

Quantity Sales- Special discounts are available on quantity purchases by corporations, associations, and nonprofits. For group discounts, contact the individual authors.

Publisher: Trendy Elite Media Group

This book is intended to provide personal growth strategies that will assist the reader in their journey. This book is not intended to provide financial, emotional health, or legal advice. Please seek appropriate counsel for financial, emotional health, or legal matters.

DEDICATION

Dedicated to the Risers – Women 45 years plus who are determined to do what's needed to thrive personally and professionally in these years. Their prime years. It's never too late to reinvent and rise.

TABLE OF CONTENTS

Foreword vii
Dr. Patricia Ramsey

Introduction 1
Dr. Alethia Tucker

Chapter 1 - The Unopened Book of Her 7
    Dr. Tabatha Russell

Chapter 2 - The Journey to My Third Act 17
    Pamela Straker, PhD

Chapter 3 - The Pivot 25
    Dr. Alethia Tucker

Chapter 4 - Interview with Dr. Barbara Williams-Skinner 33

Chapter 5 - Don't Let Your Yesterday Steal Your Tomorrow 45
    Jacqueline (Jackie) R. Scott, JD, ML

Chapter 6 - Becoming Neo 53
    Kandie Martin

Chapter 7 - Don't You Ever Give Up on Your Dream! ... 59
    Lyndia Grant Briggs

Table Of Contents

Chapter 8 - Interview with Dr. Zina Pierre 71

Chapter 9 - Reinvented with Divine Intervention 81
Pixie Lee

Chapter 10 - Morning Came, and I Was Still Alive 89
Dr. Deidra Hill

Chapter 11 - Interview with Judge Wanda Keyes Heard 99

Thank You 107

FOREWORD

As I reflect on Alethia's call about writing the foreword to her new book, I am still amazed. You may have heard the phrase, "God moves in a mysterious way, His wonders to perform," from the poem penned by William Cowper. Well, as I began to write this foreword, I heard the words, "His wonders to perform."

I was led to John 13:7, which states: Jesus replied, "You do not realize now what I am doing, but later you will understand." (NIV). What does all of this have to do with me writing this foreword? Well, you see, the person who writes a foreword generally knows the author very well; however, I only know Alethia through my sister and through Alethia's story in her book, "Reinvented to Rise." When Alethia called me, that was our first conversation on the phone ever! She knew I was very busy and would understand if I couldn't do it. God laid it on her heart to reach out to me and to write the foreword to her new book, "Reinvented to Rise, Stories of Perseverance, Strength and Courage."

Although I have never written a foreword, I found myself saying yes, as I've served as an author on scientific papers, written a book chapter on college faith, and co-authored a college textbook.

Alethia's first book, "Reinvented to Rise', gave some amazing, thought-invigorating, and powerful stories of women who reinvented themselves to rise from difficult places in life. The second volume takes another look and gives incredible perspective on what we often face as we endeavor to change. You will hear from women who overcame trying obstacles. Their challenges were incomparable and difficult; however, each one found what was needed to push through.

As women, we often find ourselves having to reinvent due to life-altering situations. When faced with one, we can reinvent ourselves to rise! To the woman who is facing a major change, maneuvering difficult circumstances, or simply in need of encouragement to pursue a dream, I recommend this book. You will be inspired. I encourage you to read the stories of eight women who reinvented themselves. Read their stories of perseverance, strength, and courage.

INTRODUCTION

Rarely does a wonderful life occur by chance? It must be made with purpose and diligence. A beautiful life necessitates the same intention and energy as a beautiful sandcastle, which doesn't just appear on the beach. Think about the evolution of a sandcastle. It takes hard work to build and real intention to make it intricate. The time taken to build it is far longer than the time required for it to wash away. The beautiful thing about a destroyed castle is that it can be rebuilt, with the newer version being stronger and more beautiful. The reinvented life is a lot like a builder determined to make a beautiful castle. She has to move forward with newfound knowledge. She has to build with the intention and energy used to build the last time and the wisdom gathered from building all the times before. This analogy best describes the woman who reinvents to rise.

Two years ago, I was blessed to lead 14 women in writing the first volume of Reinvented to Rise. The book was written during some of the most tumultuous, emotional, and challenging years that our country had ever seen. Some of the stories shared were birthed during the pandemic, while others rose from life-altering events that occurred prior to those years. I distinctly remember telling these authors that it was my desire for women reading the book to be able to see a face, story, situation, or circumstance that resonated with them. What resulted was a book full of stories of women who triumphed over situations and reinvented from different places in life. They reinvented to craft the life that they desired to have. They created full lives that allowed them to thrive as opposed to merely surviving. The original book is a little over a year old. Since publication, these authors have used

Introduction

the stories in the book to encourage change. They've taken up the mantle to pursue life in a greater place, and helped countless women do the same. However, the story did not end there.

Reinvented To Rise Volume II came to exist because of the understanding that reinvention is an iterative process and that there are many more stories to be told. As we discovered in the first book, most people go through this process more than once. This volume is no different. You will be encouraged as you hear of the processes through which identities were examined, cultural impacts were recognized, trauma was prevalent, and self-esteem frequently needed strengthening. The women in this book have shared their stories of perseverance, strength, courage, and character. I want to thank each one, for giving of themselves and embracing the belief that women can be strengthened, encouraged, and empowered by others who look a lot like them and have gone through experiences that mirror much of what they have gone through.

A special thanks to these historical Trail Blazers who lent their voices and provided profound wisdom to the reinvention discussion in this book:

Patricia Ramsey, the first Female President of Medgar Evers College

Dr. Barbara Williams-Skinner - CEO and Co-founder of Skinner Leadership Institute. She founded the Congressional Black Caucus Foundation Prayer Breakfast with her late husband, Tom Skinner.

The Honorable Judge Wanda Keyes Heard – Associate Judge, Baltimore City Circuit Court, 8th Judicial Circuit. Now retired. Judge Heard was the first woman to preside over the Baltimore Circuit Court.

Introduction

Dr. Zina Pierre - President & CEO of Reyarp Strategies Group, LLC (RSG), and pastor of Bethel Restoration Church. She served as Special Assistant to the President for Intergovernmental Affairs in the White House Executive Office of the President during the Clinton Administration. She was also the first female licensed preacher in the 150-year history of the First Baptist Church of Annapolis.

This book is for the woman who wants to get more out of life. You don't have to stay where you are if you're stuck. There is an opportunity to reinvent and rise. The stories within this book, like the others, are powerful and inspiring. The reinventions cover a broad area, and each story is followed by lessons and tips for women who desire to reinvent. Be encouraged! There is more, and it's available if you are willing to build with the intention and energy used to build the last time and the wisdom gathered from building all the times before. The best is yet to come.

Alethia Tucker

Life really is no respecter of persons, nor is reinvention. We don't know from one day to the next when our circumstances will dictate the need to change. The need to change confronts us all, no matter our appearance, our career, our history, our dialect, or our geographical location. In studying and interviewing women across educational, societal, cultural, and economic lines, I determined that there was one common thread. The common thread is survival. I discovered that it was the determination to "push through" that defined the character of the women who grace these pages. Some stories are longer, others shorter. Many have eloquently described the blows that left them breathless, while others saw more of a need to provide the bare facts, and to present them cold, hard and true.

There are women who made significant marks in history. They took bold steps that initially didn't pay off; however, their perseverance and creativity allowed them to plow through and become world-changers. They took a chance on the unimaginable and succeeded because there was no other choice.

The beauty of it all is that each story impacts differently. Each story, told from a place of authenticity, resonates with all of us in different ways. These truly are the faces of reinvention. We're all so different and yet so similar.

> *"When you have hit rock bottom and survived, there are very few things that can scare you." — **Unknown***

Dr. Tabatha Russell

CHAPTER 1

THE UNOPENED BOOK OF HER

Do you ever wonder how people bounce back from tragic loss? Books aren't just for reading; they take you to places you've never been. On this amazing journey, the book is left unopened until the very last chapter, when your eyes are opened to the full perspective of what is said to be learned. I heard a saying that made no sense and a lot of sense at the same time. If you ever want to hide anything, put it in a book because it will be the best-kept secret, never opened.

Books are such amazing tools. It hosts tons of information for the unlearned and curious to explore. But what happens when you are an unopened book? I remember being the girl who lost it all and gained everything. Have you ever wondered how people bounce back from total devastation or the feeling of hopelessness?

About the Unopened Book of Her: There comes a time when you hit a brick wall, and there's nowhere else to go. At the end of the day, when everything was gone, there was no one to call, and there was nothing else left to do but move. It seemed like it was a bad situation, but it was the blessing of a lifetime. It was during the time of my total loss that I found everything, from who I was; to whom I was called to be. In this chapter, you will learn how anyone can bounce back from anything and turn their loss into a gain if they are willing and able to let go.

You see, I was a child that grew up in inner-city Philadelphia with very humble beginnings. I was allowed to attend gifted and talented programs at a young age, which gave me exposure to people that were not like me. I grew up thinking that if I worked hard, I could acquire once admired possessions of whom I perceived to be affluent. As time went on and my life changed, I realized that these dreams would not be able to come true unless there were some major shifts in my life toward greatness.

I tried everything I could at a very young age to acquire the finer things of life, but it left me broke, busted, and defeated. I must admit, even though it was a bad situation in the beginning; it turned out to be better than good because it gave me the drive to seek out how I could make life better in the shortest amount of time for my family and me. I truly felt like the unopened book because I quickly learned nobody was coming to find out if I needed help. No one asked if I had a plan of action to bounce back. I realized that due to some of my bad choices, I had to deal with my circumstances head-on. I quickly realized I had a steep mountain to climb if I wanted things.

Once I had time to gather my thoughts after moving, I immersed myself in how to shift my mindset for prosperity. I could tap into my life's purpose, which allowed me to quickly go to work. I enrolled in college thinking that this would be the answer to help me to acquire a six-figure or higher lifestyle. I quickly learned that it would take more than that to get to where I wanted to go. I tried to become an entrepreneur, and I found hopelessness and despair. All the things I was looking for were not in a textbook. Sad to say that it took me a while to learn all the things necessary for my next level; I learned from the school of life. Don't get me wrong, college helped me chart my course, but I figured out that I needed more.

That's when I discovered that reading and investing in myself was the answer. When I learned the tools that would make me successful, it happened quicker than I ever dreamed. I learned things from my research and investing in myself that I had never even heard about in college. I learned how to channel my mindset. I learned how to be focused. I learned how to have laser-driven determination that helped me persevere at lightning speed, meaning that I created multiple businesses in a short amount of time and changed the trajectory of my family's life.

My goal went from making six-figures to creating an empire with a blueprint for others to follow to change their legacy from average to extraordinary. I've learned over the years that there are no limitations, only the ones we set for ourselves. The moment that we go beyond the stumbling blocks keeping us from our purpose is the moment that we accelerate forward. Things shift the moment that we invest in ourselves. It gives us the power to change everything. So, I encourage you to invest in yourself at the highest level possible. Remember, on your journey, don't take no for your final answer; no just means not yet. Also, don't wait for somebody to come to your rescue because, take it from me, nobody's coming to rescue you but you.

This takes me back to the day I lost everything, which was also the day I gained everything. It is interesting that hardships can teach you valuable lessons. I gained wisdom, strength, courage, and an attitude that has allowed me to persevere ever since. The curious little girl from inner city Philadelphia has learned how to overcome obstacles and fears to empower people from all walks of life around the world on how to master their endless possibilities with determination, mental clarity, and a renewed mindset being intentional and unstoppable.

A question was asked of me when others started to notice that I had shifted in my actions and business model. I quickly answered, "My perspective of success changed." Success is accomplishing an aim or purpose or attaining fame, wealth, and social status. I learned that all of the physical attributes do not measure success the physical attributes we are used to going by but by how we view success internally. I learned that I was so much further along in my journey than I realized.

Through my life's journey, I realized that I was called to be a great leader and a financial disruptor. This allowed me to focus more on the transition to serving others. I harnessed my skills in such a way that I now impact people around the country with the skills necessary for them to excel in every situation in life and in business with their finances.

I always knew that math and numbers were strengths I had possessed since I was a little girl. However, when I went through a bad business deal that caused me to lose six figures, it made me second guess my calling and, ultimately, my purpose.

When I was young, there were no conversations going on in my home about money or the importance of having a healthy relationship with money. However, I can honestly say that my mother is an excellent woman with money. I didn't realize the value of her skills and wit until I was old enough to understand how to draw strength from those around me. By this time, I had made so many mistakes it was hard to keep myself from falling off the edge of ruin. Nevertheless, the blessings far outweighed what I went through to get to where I am today.

Someone asked me, "What would I change if I had to do it all over again?"

I quickly replied, "nothing."

I believe that all of us have a path that is designed to bring us to our purpose. I might have missed mine if things had gone another way. The things I learned did not come from a textbook, and the skills I teach are a tried-and-true method that produces results. I found that I can only go so far working for someone else. You will never surpass the owner or the CEO of the corporation, which is designed to keep it that way. I knew that I wanted more, and going from employee to CEO with multiple streams of income is the path to endless possibilities. Not to mention that going after more in your life does not make you greedy but enhances your purpose.

Let me ask a few questions.

1) What would you do if you had a million dollars in disposable income?
2) Would you serve others? If so, how would you serve them?
3) What kind of Legacy do you want others to remember you by?

These are just a few questions that stared me in the face while processing some of my mistakes. Therefore, I know that we are the example that others will follow. Whether we want responsibility or not. It's not always a job we signed up for, but it becomes our reality when we are parents and caregivers full-time. My sons learned at an early age how to become resourceful through my mistakes and mindset shifts. I taught them as I learned the hard lessons.

Some hard lessons we will avoid if we listen intently to the teacher and never stop learning.

-Dr. Tabatha Russell

When we choose not to listen to sound advice, the road less traveled seems longer and more out of reach. The statistics about money are staggering. Let's look at a few facts; It is a known fact that 1 in 5 people did not save $5,000.00 in a savings or retirement account last year. An average of 63% of Americans live paycheck-to-paycheck. Then, 40% of Americans don't have $400 in their bank account to cover an emergency. Only you know if you fall into any of these categories. The decision is up to you to do something about it. Knowledge is power, and once you learn the fundamentals of wealth, you will never forget it.

There are five things that every Breakthrough Millionaire must possess in order to raise their Money Mindset:

1) Great communication. It is often said to be one of the most important qualities of a great leader is communication. It is the glue that binds an effective and productive mindset together, enabling them to function at their collaborative best. Remember, people don't know what you think most of the time unless you tell them.

2) A great leader must have the ability to recognize that every financial situation is fixable. So what you messed up along the way. At some point, even when you hit a brick wall with nowhere to go, you will have to turn around and go another way. You must be able to inspire and motivate yourself with daily affirmations, devotions, or some motivational information to condition your mindset that this, too, shall pass. Know that when you're in a less than desirable situation, it's temporary as long as you are willing to put in the work. Having confidence is contagious and motivates yourself and others to do their best. Approach every facet of your work with optimism and conviction.

3) Don't suffer in silence. So many times, that I wanted to crawl up in a ball and not deal with life. Then, I realized that I was not the only one affected by my situation. I had family that needed me, period. If you have found that you keep hitting the brick wall in your efforts, it's

time to seek support. Find yourself a coach or mentor that has done the things that you desire to do. This will allow you to accelerate your process in ways that you would not believe. Following the blueprint of a coach or mentor is priceless and life changing. Who wants to continue to struggle and fall on their face all the time? I know that I am not about that life. Be willing to invest in yourself to the highest level possible from this day forward and watch your life change in ways that you will not believe.

4) Follow the Blueprint or the System without fail. There is a reason why houses are not built until the specs of the blueprints are right. Your system should be tailored to a plan that makes sense to you, and it will assist you with accomplishing your goals. This is where you will have to be good at working hard on the things that matter the most to you and not anyone else. FOMO (Fear of missing out) is real, and it will hinder or even stop your progress if you try to keep up with the pace and momentum of others. Be ok with not being ok some days and allow yourself grace for your journey. Some days the blueprint may seem awkward. The journey is designed to get you where you desire to go. Allow time for the plan to work and stay consistent.

5) Confidence. Building wealth is a marathon and not a sprint. I wish I could say that wealth could be an overnight success for everyone. Sadly, that is one thing that you will not hear me say. Does it happen? Yes. Have the confidence that your money mindset could affect your money decisions every step of your journey. Know that there is something new to learn about money all of the time. Education is forever. Don't stop expanding your knowledge to grow your portfolio. Having this kind of confidence is needed as you now flow into realms of big purchases and being an entrepreneur. Don't slow

your progress or dim your light to make others happy. You are too valuable not to let your light shine. Your Rich Legacy awaits you. Your next financial decision could be the decision that will fill up your bank account, change or address and ultimately change your life.

Now that I have mastered the skills necessary to become a "Money Makeover Mogul ™," I have elevated my mindset, brand, and purpose. I know that every great leader is exceptional when they can empower someone else to transition effectively. I have successfully created a blueprint for others to follow to level up their Money Mindset, create multiple streams of income, and leave a rich legacy. It all started with me, then I shared my tools to empower my children first, and now I serve hundreds worldwide to walk in their confidence to live the life of their dreams unapologetically. What about you? Do you see obstacles and boundaries? Because I only see endless possibilities.

If you are having challenges and need a coach to help you navigate your journey, don't hesitate to contact me for a FREE Breakthrough Session, and follow me on social media for great financial tips and strategies.

Dr. Tabatha Russell
Website: www.DrTabathaRussell.com
FB: DrTabatha Russell ₺ Facebook
IG: Tabatha Russell (@iamdrtabatha) • Instagram photos and videos
LinkedIn: Dr. Tabatha Y. Russell ₺ LinkedIn

Dr. Tabatha Russell is a highly sought-after keynote speaker, best-selling author, and financial expert. She is arguably one of the most empowering, entertaining, and enthusiastic voices in transformational speaking today. Leveraging over 20 years of professional experience in the financial literacy industry, Dr. Tabatha is on a mission to train corporate and collegiate audiences to transform their relationship with their money so they can unapologetically give themselves permission to experience the financial freedom, stability, independence, and security they deserve.

Affectionally known as the "Money Makeover Mogul," Dr. Tabatha has become the leading authority on financial empowerment and creating environments that foster success. She challenges clients to unapologetically use their life experience and expertise to live the 6-figure life of their dreams. She mentors savvy business-women through Inside Inspired Women LLC™, a global company focused on equipping, guiding them to transition from employee to CEO of their life, business, and legacy.

Pamela Straker, PhD

CHAPTER 2
THE JOURNEY TO MY THIRD ACT

In his book, *Third Act, Reinventing Your Next Chapter*, Josh Sapan speaks of examining *"the combination of longevity and an interest in remaining relevant that not only encourages an aging population to vigorously pursue a new kind of third act but also allows them to be the "living bridge' between generations."*

Where I find myself today is not by happenstance. The journey has not been the result of a casual approach. In fact, reinvention has been a regular aspect of the journeys of my ancestors and of my own journey. As it is common to say, I stand on the shoulders of many who came before me, enabling me to benefit from their stories, experiences, and guidance. Upon reflection, there have been four distinct periods in my life.

I. Defining the Path - Developmental Years

As a young child through adolescence, I was privileged to be exposed to many people who served as "guiding lights." My parents and grandparents emphasized the importance of family, the importance of work, and the importance of "showing up" in the lives of children.

My grandparents, immigrants from Barbados, shared the stories surrounding their immigration and their reinvention as they met the challenges and demands of their new environment. In many instances, their assimilation was difficult. They talked about how they managed it. In addition to sharing their stories, they modeled behaviors that led to acquiring property, starting businesses, assuring their children were educated, managing difficult situations, and that they helped others as they went through life.

Building upon the shared knowledge of their parents, my parents made certain that I had the best education they could provide. They knew the importance of community and exposed me to people who could and would mentor me. They also taught me about the political climate in which we existed and the importance of civic engagement. They were part of local community organizations like their block association, and church, and in chapters of national organizations like the NAACP and NACW. My parents read several newspapers daily. They taught me about saving and investing money, owning property, traveling, and, most importantly, helping others. My greatest satisfaction has come from my ability to help others as I have gone through professional and life experiences.

II. Preparing to Rise - Developing and Planning Aspirations

I was an "early starter,"," finishing high school at age 15 and college at 19 and completing my doctoral studies two years later. Given my credentials as a psychologist, I was invited to work in clinical settings providing mental health services. In those settings, I was fortunate enough to be exposed to many valuable career growth opportunities, including those that enabled me to lead staff, operations, and other groundbreaking executive activities. I was on the "right track." I was always chosen to lead at the early, middle, and more advanced stages of my career. I always saw my career path as offering me the opportunity to pursue so many facets of the field.

I met each position I attained with great passion. This enabled me to work harder and to learn more because I was engaged at a deep level. As a result, those who supervised me gave me opportunities that resulted in my accomplishing and learning more than I would have if less enthusiastic.

I was licensed as a psychologist and began a private practice within two years of achieving my doctorate. In the early years of my private practice, I saw children and families earlier in my career and transitioned to seeing adults as time went on. Throughout my career, I have been called upon to speak, deliver workshops, provide psychological evaluations, serve on political advocacy panels, teach in university settings, provide clinical supervision, and develop training.

III. Practice Makes Perfect – Challenges, Successes, and Failures

In life, we all face challenges, successes, and failures. Certainly, I have faced challenges in life that resulted in successes and a few that led to failure. These experiences are of great value, and whether they culminated in success or what I consider failure, they caused me to learn so much.

I recognize that failure is not the end. Instead, I try to develop strategies to take these failures and turn them into opportunities for growth. In some cases, this may mean distancing myself from the project or whatever I've failed at to rebuild it in a new way. In other cases, it may mean acknowledging the failure, learning from it, and pushing forward into something new.

Needless to say, as my career progresses, I am more comfortable with confronting challenges and turning failures into productive learning situations. I can comfortably explore what went wrong?

What could I have done differently? How might I turn the situation around now?

I also employ what I have named the 3 "P" method for confronting challenges or urgent situations. I have used this in life and caregiving and will describe this in the next portion of this writing.

IV. Rising to the Top Revisited

I am pleased to have benefited from a long, varied, and fulfilling career. I have "been there, done that," ...except now I know what I want and need in life as I reach back to help others.

Within a field I am passionate about (health Disparities/Health Equity), I am fortunate to work with professionals for whom I have great respect. Interestingly, the thought of "retiring" had not occurred to me. I had always embraced other activities while still working. I traveled, and I enjoyed friends, music, and creative pursuits. And then came "the great retirement" resulting from the COVID pandemic. During this period, we saw unprecedented numbers of people (particularly baby boomers) retire. As I re-evaluated my own situation, there appeared to be opportunities that I could pursue.

I realized that I had a tremendous amount of information to share and that others needed more information in this area. As the population ages, there are multiple concerns about how they will navigate aging and the assistance they need. The New York Times reported in an article entitled, *The New Old Age, Who Will Care For Kinless Seniors?* that there is an increase in seniors without marital partners or family members to care for them when they need it. Increasingly, they have to seek alternative strategies and will certainly have to organize their affairs to address the period when they will need care; more information is needed on how this might be accomplished. This situation is further complicated by ever increasing costs for health care.

I had been working on the concept for a book that would share the experiences of family caregivers for some time. Given the current climate in which people are working long periods of time in their lives and confronting the need for more options concerning care as they age, I now feel compelled to contribute even more to the information that future caregivers could use to prepare for this task which would likely befall them. Remaining intellectually engaged continues to be important to me. I interviewed caregivers and worked with my book editor. While working on the book, I was fortunate to have been introduced to a coaching group that was critical to furthering my project. In 2023, I will be speaking and interviewing others on the topic of family caregiving.

One aspect of my speaking about caregiving will involve sharing my 3 "P" System that I developed in confronting urgent situations in life and in the realm of caregiving.

PAUSE: *Stop and take time to assess the situation. What is happening or has happened?*

PLAN: *Develop a Realistic Plan. What must be done to resolve the situation? Implications?*

PUT IT INTO ACTION: *Take the Steps You Have Developed in the Plan. Do it! With a timeline in effect.*

Habits for Reinvention

Throughout my life, I had found that the following habits have been beneficial and critical at times when my own reinvention was in progress:

1) Be gracious in and grateful for all life experiences and challenges and find a way to learn from those that are unpleasant. Commit to accepting and learning from your failures.
2) Embrace your history and use it to advance all that is positive, even when there are aspects you may not like. Walk in the light of those ancestors who traveled difficult roads so that your life would be better.
3) Take care of yourself physically and emotionally so that you are available to care for others.
4) Meet the challenge of urgent situations with a method to reduce stress. Use the 3 "P" System whenever you can.
5) Work hard and smartly on those things you are passionate about. In this context, seek to learn from the experiences of others.
6) Look for and embrace opportunities to help others through mentorship, fiscal support, and sharing information.

I thank you for reading this chapter and hope that it inspires you in some way.

Pamela D. Straker, PhD
E-Mail: info@drpamstraker.com.
Website: https://www.drpamstraker.com/
LinkedIn: https://www.linkedin.com/in/pamela-d-straker-ph-d-4ab5a29/
Facebook: https://www.facebook.com/profile.php?id=100085245550545.

Dr. Pam Straker is an award winning, international speaker, author, and licensed psychologist with more than 30 years of experience. She has provided psychotherapy and has managed and consulted to, nonprofit organizations and programs serving populations in which the greatest health disparities exist. She has spoken, trained, and coached in the areas of leadership, stress management, workplace conflict resolution, emotional literacy, and family-caregiving.

She currently serves as the Director of Operations for the Brooklyn Health Disparities Center (BHDC) and Research Assistant Professor, Department/College of Medicine at SUNY Downstate Health Sciences University. Her podcast, *Enduring Voices* and her book, *Heroic Caregiver, Lessons of Resilience, Coping, And Laughter* are scheduled for release in 2023.

Dr. Alethia Tucker

CHAPTER 3

THE PIVOT

We've all had something impact us. Perhaps it's an event that touches our lives in such a way that we immediately know we will never be the same. I recall one experience, and it is one that caused my life to pivot in a matter of minutes. The morning of Friday, May 9, 1980, began like any other morning. I went to the bathroom, bathed, dressed, greeted my parents, ate breakfast, and then hurriedly left the house for the bus stop. It was a beautiful, cool morning. We lived on Bolling Air Force Base (now Joint Base Anacostia) in Washington, D.C. As I walked to the bus stop, I rounded the corner and saw my friends, and, as usual, they were playing this game of making faces to force me to turn around to see who or what was behind me. This particular morning, their faces looked different. They looked perplexed and scared. Actually, they looked petrified.

I turned to look behind me, and instantly I felt the impact. I was spiraling; there was dirt, smoke, screeching, screaming, yelling, and then a thump. Everything went silent. There I was, lying flat on the asphalt. As I turned to orient myself, I saw the tire of a yellow school bus less than 1 foot away from my head. Had I been hit by a school bus?

I had absolutely no idea what I had just experienced. It felt like a huge boulder had pushed me. I couldn't breathe. I tried to see where I was hurt. I pulled myself to a sitting position. My body, from the waist down, felt like it weighed a ton. I tried to stand, but my left foot wouldn't allow me to move much at all. My foot y across my right thigh, with its bottom facing up. Although I knew I was hurt, I did not know the extent of my injuries. As sirens approached, I remained fairly calm, even through the pain of the paramedics stabilizing me to get me into the ambulance for transport to the base clinic. My parents arrived at the scene, and I believe they felt every ache and pain that my state of shock had prevented me from feeling. I looked at my father, and for the first time, I began to cry as I whispered to him, "I'm really scared."

I was transported to the base clinic, and as the shock wore off, the pain became excruciating. The medics worked hard to assess my condition and make me comfortable.

Thirty minutes into the process, one of the nurses approached me, crying. She said, "you're hurt pretty badly." I know that you're going to be ok; however, we can't do anything for you here."

With that, I began a new journey and a mentally and physically painful new norm for me.

I was taken from the clinic to the military hospital, where I was immediately rushed into surgery. Four hours later, the physician emerged and told my parents that they could get things "cleaned up," but they held very little hope for saving my foot. That summer was unlike anything my parents, or I had ever experienced.

I remained hospitalized for three months, missing the end of school and all summer. I went through a debridement process twice daily that was only made tolerable with doses of morphine. I had three operations, and the doctors offered a little more optimism after each one. They frequently stood in disbelief at the pain I could bear and the progress I had made. I faced everchanging diagnoses, from possibly losing my foot to being unable to walk. After defying the odds, again and again, one of the surgeons shared the promising thought that although they didn't know what a future prognosis looked like, I had already done far more than they initially anticipated I would be able to do.

Despite the missing bones and joints and shredded nerves and tendons, I was miraculously discharged in late July. My foot was incredibly hard to look at. I was able to walk with a severe limp. The physical scars were healing, but the emotional scars were fresh. Depression set in, and I was sad, far more than happy. One day as I sat at the kitchen table crying, I decided I would push to do better. There was so much that I could no longer do, but I wanted to be better. I went outside and started to walk with a crutch in one hand. I was in so much pain, but this became my routine. There were days when I could walk for maybe five minutes, but I did it with the neighborhood kids cheering me on. My family held me up on every side and encouraged me. My church body prayed for me fervently, but most importantly, I learned to pray for myself.

THE PROCESS

At the young age of 16, I found myself at a point of reinvention. I had to change my frame of mind and face the realization that life would move and feel different for me. This process developed my strength, perseverance, and courage. Going through such a life-altering experience required me to grow in ways I didn't know were possible. In the years following my accident, I learned I needed to push when I wanted to give up. To be badly scarred at such an impressionable age created emotional and mental challenges. As a result, I had to learn and employ processes that helped me to combat those things. Each day I faced, I had to be confident in who I was. My healing process was slow, and I had to learn to accept that I now had a new normal.

The Pivot

At this point, my reinvention needed to take place, and I had to accept where I was. In order to change the entire trajectory of my life, I had to change my mindset. I had to change the lens through which I was seeing my life in order to ensure that I in no way allowed a stained view to impact the potential that my future promised. Understanding my current state, accepting my limitations, and believing in my potential were essential steps I had to take.

Everything about the accident happened so quickly, and my mind had difficulty comprehending how I went from a teenager who was energetic and physically fit to one who was wounded and handicapped. A major shift occurred in the very activity I would do with such ease. For weeks I lie in a bed, unable to get up. Most of the time, I was heavily drugged and unable to understand much of what was happening. The doctors were so gentle with me, and they knew that my mental care was as important as my physical care. During my early days in the hospital, they told me that we would progress slowly and that I wouldn't have to look at my foot until I was ready. After weeks of avoidance, they ushered me gently into looking at the area, and at that point, I finally began to understand where I was. It was weeks into my stay at the hospital before I agreed to look at my mangled foot. The painful reality sat in over the next few weeks, and I was able to move to the next stage.

My teenage mind couldn't fathom how to navigate this handicapped place that I found myself in. I ay in the bed with uncertainty, and things didn't change when I finally left the bed. The pain that movement caused resulted in me doubting my ability to live a normal life, a life in which I would walk again, much less one in that I would be able to travel, drive or even wear normal shoes again. As time progressed, I resolved to accept my current state. Denial was sinking me into despair at a dangerous rate, and I am grateful for my parents and the medical staff that realized that I needed a support team to pull me from the abyss. And to help me to understand where I was physically so that I could begin to accept the changes that my physical state was going to bring to my livelihood. Accepting this place in life was difficult. Finally, after some time and a lot of emotional support, I could maneuver my new space and envision a way forward that accommodated where I was.

Acceptance was needed to change my view and to see that my future held potential. As I healed, I realized there were ways to work with my new limitations. Moving through life seemed more appealing, and as I became more mobile, I felt my future held promise. Whenever a setback arose, I would remember the distance I had come. In fact, future operations would frequently require that I repeat the entire stage of awareness and acceptance. The goal was always to move forward. My mindset change enabled me to make it through. I was able to reinvent and refine my view so that I could embrace a future that held promise.

THE PROMISE

As an adult, I realized that my experience during a traumatic time in life taught me my first lesson in reinventing. The trauma I experienced initially caused me to doubt that my future held the promise I envisioned. The support I received in handling my trauma was critical, and my decision to accept my physical limitations truly changed the trajectory of my life. My early years introduced me to the mindset change tools I now use. These tools were instrumental in developing the strategy that I employ when helping women navigate life in the mid stages.

That critical day in May caused a major pivot in my life that led me to a painful process. That process helped me to refocus and view my life with the proper perspective. That perspective, once cleared, revealed the promising future that had always been available. The trauma I experienced also solidified lessons that I use to ensure that my life reflects the greatness that God has always desired for me. What follows are lessons I've learned during my reinvention process. I know these lessons will also prove beneficial for you.

You are resilient. You may buckle, but that doesn't mean you will break.

I realized that I could go through rough times, and the pain can be excruciating and, at times, debilitating. When I was hospitalized, I went through pain that even the strongest morphine drip couldn't soothe. The fact that I would go through the pain time and time again and realizing that experiencing repeated pain was necessary for my healing is a true testament to what I can endure. That experience reminds me that there will be periods in life when I will need to bend. The key is to remember that I don't have to break in the process, but I need to be flexible.

You can't let negative probabilities negate the promising possibilities that exist in your life.

I've learned that my possibilities far outweigh any negative circumstances that could occur in my life. When I entered the operating room, the surgeons had a diagnosis of doom hanging over my life. I could have given up on their probabilities, but I chose not to. For weeks they had no idea what to expect. Once I began to do the work around shifting my mindset, I embraced what could possibly happen. When the thoughts of amputation reared up, I pushed harder to do all of the necessary things to facilitate healing. My parents helped by surrounding me with positivity. The positivity came from books, music, visitors, and any other creative venue they could conjure up to elevate my spirits. Those were the things that helped me to persevere, and they helped me to maintain a posture of hope. Negativity can't be allowed to take residence in the mind. I hold onto the promises that God has for me and I do what's needed to reinforce my belief that better is in store for me.

There are times when you may have to look back, but if you miss the opportunity to do so, don't let it stop you from moving forward.

There was a time when I frequently thought of "what if." What if I had turned around earlier when I heard something behind me? What if I rode into the district with my parents that morning? Would my life have changed? Would I have gone through such a painful process? I stopped asking myself that question when I realized that, looking back could have caused greater trauma, or even worse, it could have caused my death. I have released my speculation. There are going to be times when it's necessary to reflect on life. We may need to look back at lessons learned. I fully believe in the importance of your story in every aspect of growth in your life. There may be times when I'll remember to look back, and then there may be times that I forget. It's ok either way. Even in suffering the repercussions of not grabbing those lessons, I have to remember that God will ensure that every bit of my life will work for my good. My job is to have the courage to push and not let anything keep me from moving forward.

Dr. Alethia Tucker
www.joleaseenterprises.com
atucker@joleaseenterprises.com
Instagram: @alethiaatucker and @joleaseenterprises
Facebook: Alethia Tucker and Jolease Enterprises
LinkedIn: Coach Alethia Tucker

Alethia Tucker is a highly sought-after international keynote speaker, reinvention strategist, and bestselling author. Regarded as one of the most influential voices of motivational speaking, Alethia impacts audiences worldwide with her message of encouragement and empowerment.

Alethia has over 20 years of human resources, training, and marketing experience. Alethia founded Jolease Enterprises, which offers strategies for reinvention by overcoming self-limiting thoughts, doubt, and fear. She also hosts the Reinvent and Rise Show and Leveling up the Podcast.

As an influential figure, she serves as a visionary of an anthology and an Amazon #1 bestselling author of five books: 50 Things I've Learned on My Way to 50, Women Crushing Mediocrity, Speaking My Truth, and Reinvented to Rise and Daddy's Girl. Alethia's work has been featured on prominent media platforms such as ABC, CBS, NBC, FOX, and in leading magazines, newspapers, podcasts, and news articles, including Yahoo Finance, Boston Herald, and New York Weekly.

CHAPTER 4

INTERVIEW WITH DR. BARBARA WILLIAMS-SKINNER

CEO and Co-founder of Skinner Leadership Institute. Co-Founder of the Congressional Black Caucus Foundation Prayer Breakfast.

Dr. Tucker: Dr. Williams-Skinner, thank you so much for being here today and agreeing to interview with me. What better way to help women than to bring in someone like yourself, who is a history maker and someone who has had experience in making changes and enabling change to occur?

Dr. Williams-Skinner: Thank you so much for having me.

Dr. Tucker: Why don't you tell us a little about yourself and what you're doing right now?

Dr. Williams-Skinner Okay. I am a sixties child who grew up in the San Francisco Oakland, Richmond Bay area in the sixties. Kind of impacted by the Black Nationalist movement more than the Civil rights movement. Raised by an amazing mother of eight, no father who, despite our great poverty, always encouraged me to pursue my passion for education. I talked very early about becoming an advocate for the poor, low-income families like mine. Three or four advanced degrees later, I became the first female executive director of the Congressional Black Caucus with such luminaries and trailblazers working with Shirley Chisholm, Barbara Jordan, Andrew Young, and so many others. And so, for the past 30 years, most of my time and attention has been on creating a just and equitable world with a lot of different partners.

I was an agnostic for most of my early life until almost 40; as you know, two of my books really connect those faith things to me. I consider myself an advocate for the underserved. What am I doing now? That's the work that I'm doing. I am the CEO and President of Skinner Leadership Institute. We equip leaders for high-character leadership. Leadership doesn't have to be a high character. We have a lot of low-character leaders. We have a world filled with them, and violence and division are the result of that.

So, we do that on purpose, whether it's members high level, well-known leaders, I'll just say, or millennial Gen X leaders. We do master series for distinguished younger leaders, six months of the year, from all over the country. We equipped clergy for public policy. More recently, I've been coordinating ten state voter protection campaigns for the midterm election, which will continue for 2024. That's the work that I did.

Dr. Tucker: That's great. That is definitely trailblazing. It really is. I hear what you're passionate about, and I love that you are doing things across the spectrum for leadership and helping millennials and helping those who are established to need to get more in depth and actually more skilled in being leaders. Is there anything else that you're passionate about? I think I've heard most of it.

Dr. Williams-Skinner: Yes, I'm passionate about young people. I'm really passionate about young people walking in their power and not just those who want to become public policy leaders, but whether they want to become business leaders or owners or

Interview With Dr. Barbara Williams-Skinner

whatever, that this generation has a lot of information, but not all the wisdom that they need. I'm passionate about sports. I think you have to have a little football in particular. You need a balanced life. I find ways to not make all of my life just about work because I think a leader who's out of balance is not the best leader.

Dr. Tucker: Exactly. I love you said that because in our lifetime, I know in mine, I've seen leadership where it's been well-balanced and where it really hasn't been well-balanced. I've seen organizations really suffer because of it. So, I love to hear that balance is a piece of that equation that you include.

Dr. Williams-Skinner: It's a struggle. I've conquered that. I think that's an aspiration every single day.

Dr. Tucker: I think we all do, particularly in this world where things are just it seems to be getting faster paced, more detailed, is what I like to call it. I appreciate the fact that balance is a big part of what you advocate for.

Dr. Williams-Skinner: I'm also excited about women in non-traditional leadership positions. Women leaders in general. I was so excited about helping to advocate for Ketanji Brown Jackson to be the first black woman on the Supreme Court. For younger women coming into Congress right now, of the nine new members of the Congressional Black Caucus, the majority are females, and they're under 40. I have a heart for young women in leadership positions because I think women leaders have a harder way to go in their leadership positions.

Dr. Tucker: Absolutely. You've indicated the things you really have your footprint in. And so, you've worked with women across all spectrums. What have you really seen in all the work that you've done? What have you found that career women really need the most? Where is the most support they need when endeavoring to make a change?

Dr. Williams-Skinner: There are several things that women need when trying to make a change. One is they need faith. They need a spiritual base because there are so many obstacles to their entering the C-suite or the highest rank of the ladder everywhere. So, you must be rooted and grounded in something bigger than yourself. You need support systems. There's no such thing as an effective lone ranger. I've never seen one. So, you need people who got your back, who don't want anything from you, who aren't just doing the atta girl when things go well, but they're like, they're with you when things don't go well, and they're there to help pick you up in case things go south. You also need to have, an honest perspective of your own strengths and weaknesses.

Just because you're in the position doesn't mean you have to be the bionic woman. You have to understand where you're really good and where you need support and be willing to get people around you who may be better than you at certain tasks. So, you need a team. I think the other thing is you need allies. You need to know where you need people outside your comfort zone. If you're a Democrat, maybe you need some Republican leaders. I mean, moderate Republicans, of course. If you're a black woman, you definitely need to have some white men and women and people of different races and backgrounds who are on your side, whom you can partner with consistently. I think because African Americans are under siege so much, you will have to have people you can partner with in the trenches.

I think that's the other tool you need. And then you need to have some people you can have fun with. People you can just have no agenda time with. Again, I think you need some life-work balance. Women are having heart attacks at the same rate as men because we don't care for ourselves. We take care of our families, and we take care of our church or our organization, but often we don't take care of ourselves. So, you need a wellness plan; that's what you need. A plan for life-work balance. I think those are some of the things that women on the top need.

Dr. Tucker: Yeah, that's one I haven't mastered. We've talked about the things that women need to have with them as a toolkit, so to speak when they're trying to implement change. Was there a point, and I'm sure there has been? Would you like to tell us about a point in your life where you felt that you had to reinvent yourself in any way?

Dr. Williams-Skinner: Absolutely. I've had to reinvent myself over the years, probably three different times. First, I reinvented myself from an agnostic to a woman of faith. That was big. The people I related to, the people I got to know, and the people I listened to were very different. What I didn't know could fill volumes. So, I had to learn what I didn't know and to know that I didn't know what I didn't know in the face field. My husband was an evangelist but married a woman who barely knew the difference between Genesis and Revelation. So that was the first reinvention. Most of my friends previously were political. So now, a whole group of people in the faith community added to that. Within that community, very diverse Republicans, Democrats, Black, Asians, Latinos, and Whites.

So that was a whole new way of thinking. Reinvention is about rethinking yourself. It's about thinking differently about your options and your opportunities. The second, of course, was being second in command to my husband, the president of Skinner Leadership Institute. I was a vice president until he passed away. I loved being number two. I didn't have a problem with that. I loved working on the vision and making it work behind the scenes. It was traumatic for me, to say the least, to now hear my board say, you're now our president and CEO. Okay. That was a whole new thing for me. So I had to think differently about how my words mattered. They carried weight. I represented an organization. I just couldn't go on my feelings. I had to have more facts.

I had to be backed up by research and facts. I had to think about the people I partnered with, the relationships I built, and the like. So that was different. I had a different way of thinking, and now I'm responsible in a different way. So the third way is now, as an elder Stateswoman, thinking about myself more as a teacher and a trainer and a coach, a live coach to younger women, which is what I'm doing right now. The Master series for Distinguished Leaders is a program that we built about 15 years ago. In fact, this is our 15th year thinking about how you create a farm team for the next generation of Shirley Chisholm and Barbara Jordans, the next generation of Mary McLeod Bethune, the next generation of people like Andrew Young and John Lewis. And we do that two days a month, beginning January to June.

It allows me to be in touch with young minds and sharp minds. They come from corporations, governments, nonprofits, IT, and other places. It's all by interviews. So we only select 15 a year because it's very focused. We coach them up. They have an assigned mentor. They do community service. I don't care what position they're in. We gotta work with the underserved, with gun violence victims, and others. So that is a program that we fashion after our own lives to say, how did we get here? We didn't just hatch as organizers. So, we have a curriculum, we have the training, and we invite them to Capitol Hill or meet with members of Congress and other high-level leaders. So, I am enjoying this current phase of my life probably even more because I'm watching these young people. They're filled with hope and brightness, yet they may not have all of the tools for dealing with strategic issues or dealing with systemic racism in the same way.

They may not be involved in the same overt racism that some of my generation and others, but they're facing glass ceilings that they're not prepared for and microaggression on their jobs. That's maybe a bit more subtle, but nevertheless hurtful that they must prepare for. We talk about those things in confidential settings in the master series for distinguished leaders. So, I'm enjoying this new reinventing phase of my life as a stateswoman.

Dr. Tucker: It's funny because I always tell people reinvention is continuous. It's not like you do it one time in life, and that's it. You reinvent as life changes, and as the years go by and you have had some phenomenal things going on that you have reinvented for, just absolutely phenomenal. What would you say are the tools that you recommend women have? What do they want to hold onto when endeavoring to reinvent, either personally or professionally?

Dr. Williams-Skinner: You then need to understand your "why." Like, why am I pursuing this? You have to have passion. What is your passion? If you don't have passion for something, when you get obstacles, when you face obstacles, you're going to back down. So, you've got to understand, why am I in this battle? Why am I pursuing this? Be really clear about your own motives. Is this because I want attention? Do I want to just be seen and be among those who are seen, or am I committed beyond that, whether I'm seen or not? I think you also need to know who your real friends are. Some people, when you get into the limelight, or not even necessarily in the limelight, but you get to a high position, the attacks come with that as well. Jealousy. People ask how did she get to be invited to the White House? As I am a lot, invited to capital. How do you get to meet with members of Congress on a regular day? What does she have that

Interview With Dr. Barbara Williams-Skinner

I don't have? So, you get the comparison. I think the woman trying to make it to the top needs to be clear about who she is. Who her friends are. And thirdly, I'm talking now not about external tools. I'm talking about internal tools. You have to be really comfortable with who you are.

Really comfortable. You're not comparing yourself to anybody. God made you so unique that the iris of your eye, and your footprint is so different from everybody else. God knows every hair on your head. There's nobody like you. When God made you, he was so amazed at you that he just quit. So, the idea of comparing myself to another woman's looks or whatever she has is absurd. I'm telling God that he messed up. So, she's gotta be comfortable in her own skin. I think the other thing is that the need for external affirmations needs to stop. You need to begin to get up every day and affirm yourself. If you are a seeker after relationships because you need people to affirm you, high-level positions are not for you because the higher up you go, the less of that you'll get. Don't make a mistake.

Have more of the internal strength, character, integrity, the ability to be empathetic when people are down, to never get so high up that you can have to ask how did you get in that position? Always be prepared to say, how can I help you? Sometimes, it even helps to remember when you weren't "all that." Remember the battles that you had to go through to get there. I'm really talking more about internal strength because I think the external strength you can get, you can get the ability, you can learn how to speak well and preach well and teach well. Those are externals. You can learn how to manage well. You can even get leadership skills. The internal strength the woman trying to do breakthrough work mostly comes from within.

Dr. Tucker: Wow! Those are powerful tools, power tools. I love the affirmation piece and understanding that God made you unique. It's something that I also say is your imprint; no one else has that. The fact that women need to be more focused on that, I think that is a huge piece of where we really start to fall into the self-esteem issues when we just try to compare to what society says we need to look like. As you said, basically telling God you've messed up. I'm really not good enough.

Dr. Williams-Skinner You have to know that God values you and that you are more than enough.

Dr. Tucker: Every day, we all need that. Well, thank you so much for talking to me today. Again, I want to thank you for being one who has paved the way so that women such as myself can do the things that I do. I realize that if it had not been for women doing the things and making the imprints you have made, my way would be even more challenging than it is now. We both know that we still have a little ways to go, but the inroads that you have made have benefited me and so many others, and I thank you for that.

Dr. Williams-Skinner: You're very welcome.

"The most important journey of our lives doesn't necessarily involve climbing the highest peak or trekking around the world. The biggest adventure you can ever take is to live the life of your dreams."
Oprah Winfrey

To truly be happy, you have to follow your dreams. That sounds so simple to say and yet so complicated to walk out. Life has a tendency to hit hard and sometimes those blows result in injury. Those injuries cause us to doubt, fear and believe that we are not capable of attaining those things that we desire with all of our hearts. If we're not careful we'll tuck those desires away and not follow up on our possibilities.

The world is full of challenges and obstacles to our dreams. In order to push past these difficult places, you have to believe that it's possible to get beyond them. The women in this book have managed to do just that. For some dreams were halted by trauma and for others, dreams were paralyzed by the witness of seeing others miss opportunities over and over again. These women still pulled and pushed to dispel what life had illustrated before them, determined to change the trajectory of their lives. They rose above the circumstances and decided to take a chance on the very things that grasped at their souls.

In these pages you will hear stories of those living in their prime years and endeavoring to make their mark in bettering healthcare for the aging. You'll hear from trailblazers who moved from positions of unbelief to organizing successful communities around faith. You'll hear from a daughter who is determined to follow through on her dreams and the dreams of the ones who paved the way before her. You'll see how a rise from a fall can yield lessons that are instrumental in demonstrating a process to reinvent life.

In a society where many are settling to live out life in mediocrity, these women have placed themselves in position to soar. Be encouraged by what you hear. Whatever your story, don't allow yourself to dismiss the desires of your heart.

It is said that to do something well you must enjoy it. Doing what you love, and going after a big dream can be complicated. See how these women dared to move, putting faith and hope at the forefront. When we operate from this space, we allow space for miracles in our lives, because we believe in the possibility of it.

Jacqueline (Jackie) R. Scott, JD, ML

CHAPTER 5

DON'T LET YOUR YESTERDAY STEAL YOUR TOMORROW

"You stand between two thieves...your yesterday and your tomorrow." Dr. Tony Evans

MOM

My mother died of a broken heart, literally and figuratively. For years she carried with her the weight of unfulfilled promises and broken dreams. We buried my mother with her dreams inside of her. Since that day, I've secretly walked in fear of the same happening to me yet determined to write a different chapter for my life.

When a woman loses her mother, it changes her. Nothing is the same. Since my mother's passing, I've been in a battle *with* myself in search of myself. Searching to find my voice, to connect the dots to seemingly unconnected memories, and to reconcile tangled emotions and feelings.

ME

When first approached about sharing my story my first reaction was "there's nothing so remarkable, memorable, or life-changing about my life worthy of a chapter in this book, why choose me?". Yet I realize it's just that kind of thinking that's kept me bound, quiet, hiding in the shadows of myself...voiceless, seen but not truly being seen.

I learned at a very early age to hide in plain sight. If you're the oldest child or the oldest girl in the family, some of what I say next will sound very familiar. I worked hard to be the "good one," the responsible one who took care of everyone else and lived up to everyone's expectations. I was the overachiever who dared not disappoint. I took on responsibilities way too big for me and was steadfastly determined to solve problems that weren't mine to solve. I became the pleaser who tried to make everyone happy.

US

In many ways, my mother and I grew up together. She was only 18 when she had me. I watched her struggle, grow, and yearn deeply for the achievements she was on the way to before me. I heard her tears. Rarely saw them, but I heard them. As a young child I would listen and watch everything. I was a curious one. I took in everything around me. Having me at 18 disrupted her dreams and caused her great shame. But it didn't destroy her. She was resilient, determined, and strong.

She was a proud woman, the oldest of two daughters my grandparents would have. She herself would ultimately become the beloved mother of four. She took care of us, of everything, while tucking away her dreams. Always externally put together, pouring into us, while taking care of others. From the outside, successful to all, she would light up a room. Later as an adult, I learned she struggled with an emptiness, a yearning inside to fill the broken places. It wasn't until after I lost her and started to "do my work" to reconcile my grief that I realized I was doing the same thing. You see, we grew up together.

What I have come to understand is that somewhere in my seven- or eight-year-old self, her tears became mine. They became my fuel, pushing me into what would become "solve it," "fix it," and "pleaser" mode. As a young adult, it somehow evolved into "this won't be me" mode. That's when I began running from myself. Masterfully dancing between shame and praise. I had no idea for years what to call this dance or even how to describe it. It was just something I did with ease, like second nature, because it was in me, in my mother.

My mother carried the shame of having me as an unwed teen in the 60s. As a child, I was too young to comprehend the true impact it had on her. Yet I sensed something. The kitchen table conversations, the whispers, those conversations grown folks have that make your ears perk up even though you know you are not supposed to be listening. Grown folks' business. I realize now that I subconsciously internalized what everyone thought they were keeping from me. Growing up, I often wondered, was I good enough? Was I enough? Was I always going to be in the shadows of the circumstances of my birth?

Later in life, my mother would share glimmers of the internal weight of the shame she carried because of the pregnancy. She felt she disappointed her parents, family, teachers, and friends. She revealed that as an 18, 19, 20+-year-old new mom, she battled internally with the same questions of self-worth I did without even knowing it. Soul ties and generational trauma are real.

And yet there I was, fully loved, embraced, and praised from my earliest memories. I grew up surrounded by so much love and care. Mixed in with all that love were everyone's dreams and expectations. It felt as if everyone just transferred them from my mother to me. My mother's deferred dreams and my grandparents' once-denied now renewed dreams all rolled up into a nice, neat bundle of expectations for me. I know they didn't mean any harm. They LOVED me deeply. I never knew anything less than full, uninhibited love. So, for me, disappointing them was not an option. I had to prove to everyone that I could fulfill their dreams, the ones THEY had for me. I went into overdrive. Overachiever on steroids - Homecoming Queen, Miss. Debutante, graduating 2nd in my high school class, attending a top-tier university despite being told by my guidance counselor that I "would never get in." Embarking on a college experience where I tried to embed myself in almost every facet of the place that I could. Ultimately getting three degrees from that institution.

Determined not to disappoint. Head down, checking boxes, professional achievements, taking care of business. Making people proud. All the while never "checking in" with myself. Why? Because I was "all good." I was handling the pressures of life, taking the ups and the downs, and taking care of my people. I was there for folks who needed me. I was the dependable one.

I know now that I was not "all good." I had simply mastered hiding in plain sight. I'd learned so early how good the love and the praise felt each time I met or exceeded expectations that I just did things out of habit, discounting whether it was really something I wanted or not. Most of the time, it was just what I thought I was supposed to do. But I liked the feeling of pleasing, so I just kept tucking my*self* deeper and deeper inside.

How could I possibly complain? Who would have any sympathy or empathy for a well-educated, seemingly accomplished, pretty much drama-free, and well-liked person like me? How do you tell people you feel empty, unfulfilled, and unseen? How do you step out of shame and fear to admit you've been living in a shadow of yourself?

MY JOURNEY TO RISE

My mother and I had many breakthroughs the last two years of her life, yet I desperately needed more time. She was intensely private and very proud. She'd just begun sharing her story... our story when I lost her. She left me with more questions than answers and, thankfully, more courage than fear. Armed with the courage and perseverance to push past the shadows of myself and to fully embrace the voice I've suppressed for so long; I am rising.

My journey to rise has taken on three phases:

Phase 1: Remember and Review: We cannot rise from which we cannot identify. We must be willing to dig deep, identify and clearly name it. Just talking about emotion (pain, disappointment, fear, etc.) is not enough. We must be willing to dig deep into the memories and identify the incident, action, person, etc. Be as specific as possible and stay with that memory. Challenge yourself, dissect the memories, sit with them, and give them your full review until you have true clarity. It wasn't until I took the time to sit with the memories, I had of 7, 8, 9-year-old Jackie that I truly had a breakthrough.

Phase 2: Refocus and Reconnect: It's hard to admit, but when searching for answers to our pain we often move too quickly and focus on the wrong thing or the wrong person. We just want the pain to go away. I was so focused on happiness – making others happy and finding my own happiness, that I totally missed the truth. I was empty. Being empty and being happy are very different. Happiness can be fleeting, momentary. Emptiness grows, deepens, and festers. My problem was not that I was unhappy, it was that I'd spent so much time pouring out and into others that there was a numbness deep inside, a place of unfulfillment that left me yearning for more. Had I stayed focused on achieving "happiness," I don't believe I would have changed. I would have simply continued to hide in plain sight, just with a smile on my face. We must be willing to challenge ourselves to direct our energy to the things in and about us that are not so easy to see. We must stay open to new revelations and look for how those revelations connect us to who we were, who we are, and whom we desire to become.

Phase 3: Re-energize for Rebirth: Rising from places of pain and discontent takes courage, perseverance, determination, and commitment. Work is involved, and you will need the energy to accomplish it. As I continue to work through this phase, I've realized that my life does not have to be a set of binary choices, no "either ors." I can do and be many things. I can fulfill my calling to help others find their voices while cultivating and elevating my own. I can see myself in the mirror and acknowledge that I deserve to be heard and seen as me. I always equated doing things for myself as selfish acts because I thought I had to be selfless, humble, and hidden. The supporter, the helper, the dependable one. I created a narrative that was not true. One that kept me shrinking inside, away from my authentic, God-given power.

There is a spiritual place inside of you that you must call upon on your journey to rise. A place that you must tap deep inside. One where you acknowledge there is a God force bigger than you. It will help you see that you are worthy, deserving, and worth fighting for. You are God's masterpiece, fearfully and wonderfully made.

Put yourself in the posture for rebirth. It is truly like labor. Breathe and push through. Steady yourself in expectation and be prepared for a move of God in your life. Allow yourself to awaken to a new you, with new opportunities, new callings, and the freedom to dream your own BIG dreams. Today, together, our rebirthing has begun. We will RISE.

Jacqueline (Jackie) R. Scott, JD, ML
LinkedIn: Jacqueline Belk Scott
Contact: expressurself247@gmail.com

Guided daily by her faith, Jackie adopted Isaiah 50: 4-7 as her life scripture. Wherever possible she uses her voice in both her professional and personal pursuits to empower and improve the lives of women, children, and the most vulnerable among us. Jackie is a seasoned executive known for her strong leadership, people, and strategic skills. Trained in both law and business she has successfully used her skills to build and achieve results with cross-functional, local, national, and global teams. Jackie has successfully worked in government, non-profit, and business sectors, gaining a reputation for using creativity and innovation to make decisions, problem solve, and develop strategies that deliver outcomes with measurable results. She holds a dual BA from Georgetown University; a Juris Doctor from the Georgetown University Law Center; a Master's in Leadership from the McDonough School of Business at Georgetown; and studied Pastoral Counseling at Loyola University. Jackie lives in Howard County with her husband and three children.

Kandie Martin

CHAPTER 6
BECOMING NEO

So let me tell you about my best 50th birthday present. Want to know what it was? I lost my job. Now I know some of you are like, "Kandie, oh my God, that is not a gift", but before I go through why I think it was a gift, let me explain who I am.

My name is Kandie Martin. I'm a social butterfly who has been in business for over 13 years. Let me tell you about the first ten years. My business was just a side chick. When I say on the side, Chile, I mean on the side and being dusty. And I only did it when I felt like it. I didn't worry about the business making money, it was just there, something extra to do. Everyone in my family has a side business, so I was doing something that I was familiar with. They all have a regular 9 to 5 job, and their business is on the side. For the last three years, I have been a 100% Entrepreneur and running a profitable business. I am a multi-media strategist. I help people and businesses excel in the media. My main focus is social media, where I help small to medium sized businesses rock their social media just like fortune 500 companies.

Back to my story. On January 15, 2019, I lost my job. My six-figure job. When I say, I was devastated, oh my God. I couldn't get out of bed for a couple of days. For the first two months, I was just going through it. I was going through everything. 401K, stock, savings, and the list goes on. Everything was used up as I was trying to stay afloat. On top of that, I had to make a decision. Do I keep my house, or do I keep my car? Do I try to find a job to keep the car? I had to make a decision. I made the decision to let my car go and use my daughter's car while she was at work. So, again, I'm still going through it. Trying to drive for Lyft around my daughter's schedule while still trying to find a job, all of my efforts were blocked. I was getting up every morning, applying for every job opening there was, then turning on the Lyft app and trying to make money. When I say no one would hire me; even McDonald's wouldn't hire me. I was either overqualified or underqualified. You see, I don't have a degree. I dropped out of college when I had my first child; life happened, and things went from there. But that's a whole other story we won't get into.

I had to start believing in myself because I am Neo. And if any of you have watched the Matrix, the first one, in my opinion the best one, you probably understand just what I mean. When Neo started believing in himself, he could dodge bullets. Now I ain't trying to dodge bullets, and I'm not saying that I can. However, God gives us gifts, and some of us have multiple gifts. And with that gift, we have to believe in the gift we are given and work that gift as if our life depends on it. In my case it did!

At the end of 2019, I sat down and made my plan. I knew I had this business, making a few dollars, and people were asking me to run their social media. So, I thought, "Let's figure this out." I started by looking at all of my bills, to include household and business bills. I came up with the amount that I had to earn in order for me to survive. That was imperative because I knew that driving Lyft all day was not going to be my life. Once I figured how much I needed to earn, I had to determine the cost of my packages, and the number of different packages I would have. Once I settled on three packages and what I would offer in each of the packages, I had to figure out the prices. I came up with my magic number of clients, ten. I then divided the amount of money I had to make by ten, this became my base package amount. Each tier up from the base was an additional one hundred dollars. With that, I had my packages! Next, I booked a speaking engagement, and during that speech, I figured that I would be able to pitch my offer. January 2020, I nailed the speaking engagement and did my best pitch. I had over 20 people to schedule time on my calendar. When I signed up my first five clients at my base rate, I retired that amount, and my new base rate was my second-tier rate. I started working on my plan, believing in myself, and trusting that God had me. Once I started doing that, by March 2020, I was completely straight and out of the hole. The pandemic hit, and I got more business. I went from making $1000 a year in my business to over $65,000 in one year! I continue the same plan to this day; once I get five people paying my base rate, the rate goes up by $100.

I now offer all types of marketing, not just social media, and I help my clients with their websites and email marketing. I even have my own social media posting system and an all-in-one system. I partnered up with some more entrepreneurs and created a television network. Completely working on making my client's businesses be seen and heard not just online but in person as well. I learned how to S.I.T. in my business. This stands for Strategic partnerships, interns, and technology. This enables my business to offer services that my clients need without me having to perform all of the services. This also helps me to continue to perform better and faster with my services. In addition to all of this, I help other entrepreneurs do what I did, come up with their packages and plans so that they can become more successful.

Life is a never-ending cycle of reinventions, and the one I have described is one of the most meaningful transformations that changed the direction of my life. Now you see why I say my best birthday present was losing my job because it made me focus on my business. Now I am making the same amount of money from my business that I was making in corporate America, and now I am "unfireable." I say this because people can stop using my company's services, but they can't stop me from being me.

So, what are my tips for you if you face a time when you must reinvent? First, I want you all to remember what I said in my story. When you get into a bad place, don't think you don't have to be upset. It's perfectly normal to be upset about what you're losing, but don't let the loss devastate you to where you can't go forward. You have to believe that there is more outside of what you lost. Be upset, cry, and lay in bed for a couple of days if you have to. But when you get finished, get yourself together. Secondly, make sure you pray and create and write down a plan and make it plain. The Bible talks about writing down the vision. Something happens when you write down the vision. You can devise the best way to meet your goals. Recording the vision also helps you to get clear on exactly what you want to do. I knew that if I stuck to my vision, I stood a better chance of going in the right direction to get the desired results.

Third, work your plan like your life depends on it because it does. You have to be laser focused. You cannot give up when hurdles come. Consistency and perseverance are critical to your success. I talked about Neo at the beginning of my story. As the main character of the movie many believed in Neo, but he did not believe in himself. He tried but failed and believed that he would not be able to succeed. Initially, he wasn't sure of his powers, even though he could do things that others could not do. Once Neo believed in his ability, he was able to accomplish anything! You have to do the same. Believe in yourself, keep learning, and never stop trying. This is how I became Neo, and so can you!

Kandie Martin
Website: kandieenterprises.com
Contact: ask.kandiemartin.com

Instagram: @kandieenterprises
LinkedIn: Kandie Martin

Kandie Martin is a Georgia native, moving to Atlanta in 1997. She put her modeling career on hold and started in the Information Technology field working in that field for over 20 years. She started her first business in 2009 based off her poetry and Poems by Kandie was born. The company was reinvented into a personal assistant company. In 2015, she revamped the company again and Leave It To Kandie, LLC started managing comedians and actors. 2019 she started her magazine and modeling agency. In 2020, she started concentrating on the social media management portion of her company and Kandie Enterprises was birthed and all her companies are now under one roof. Kandie has been nominated for ATL Hottest Manager, winner of URBAN CEO Most Talented CEO (2019) and recipient of Urban CEO Founders Award for 2020, and author of several books.

Lyndia Grant Briggs

CHAPTER 7

MOVING FORWARD AFTER THE LOSS

Reinventing yourself is like the metamorphosis of a butterfly; you crawl on your belly, and you live in a cocoon. Finally, you become a beautiful butterfly!
Lyndia Grant

JESSIE L. JACKSON'S OFFICIAL' BRONZE BUST UNVEILED

Anxious and ready to work in the new family business, adrenalin was still running in high gear from our big '*grand opening celebration*' recently held. It was a dream come true when Critique Career Management Services, Inc. (Critique), a new company with four sisters serving as the board of directors, came together as entrepreneurs to open this small business. Over the years, we became known as The Grant Sisters of Georgia Avenue throughout the Washington, DC Area. We hit the ground running. We are ready, willing, and delighted to help our community by providing a career management service.

I was a supervisor in the Nursing Administration Office at Children's Hospital Medical Center, Oakland, California. My role as the 'head' Search & Selection Manager taught me so much that I felt compelled to share my knowledge with other African Americans. In the scriptures, what happened to me, felt like the story of Saul, a man who God called to do a great work for his people. A spiritual light was shined down on him, and he became Paul; this is the best example to show how this calling was upon my life. I was thankful that my sisters were willing to join me. Ernestine was a college student, having recently completed a term in the U.S. Army, Franquis, worked at 20th Century Fox in Los Angeles, and Jakki Grant had recently left the Bay Area. She moved back home to Washington, DC. She worked at Design Three, another family-owned engineering and design company. We came together to work as a family and planned a grand opening to remember.

Being led by a vision that worked out perfectly, in my subconscious mind, I could see the sign that Dr. Martin Luther King, Jr. and his Civil Rights marchers carried; it said ***"Jobs, Peace & Freedom."*** As if I was answering the call to help folks get jobs, I felt led to invite our keynote speaker, a Member of Congress for the District of Columbia, The Honorable Walter E. Fauntroy, D.C. Delegate. He had been a founding member of the Student Non-Violent Coordinating Committee (SNCC), seen during the 1960s working with Dr. Martin Luther King, Jr.

This new business was our chance to help in our own way. Therefore, our grand opening was February 11, 1983. It was our goal to help our community get jobs by offering resume writing services, preparing job campaigns, and teaching customers effective job search techniques and strategies, as I had learned from my work at the Children's Hospital in Oakland.

What made our grand opening so special was our 'A' list of dignitaries. Councilmembers, Honorable Charlene Drew Jarvis, Ward 4 area, and Honorable Nadine P. Winter, Ward 6. The Master of Ceremonies was a daily news correspondent from NBC 4, Fred Thomas.

Though we were unknowns, we garnered some 'heavy hitters' who said yes, and they attended our opening ceremonies.

Moving Forward After The Loss

After the success of our opening and newspaper articles in a couple of local papers, we had hoped this publicity would help to put us on the map and customers would come knocking.

However, within a few weeks after the opening, I couldn't help but notice our phone wasn't ringing. The only calls we got were from friends and family. We had a problem. If our goal was to reinvent ourselves from former sharecroppers' daughters to rise to become entrepreneurs, something else had to happen. We had to find new ways to market our resume writing services and do it quickly! The rent had to be paid! Back in the 1980's businesses had brick-and-mortar office spaces.

We put our heads together to figure things out. We needed influential mentors and networking experiences to help us discover what we did not know. None of us had run a small family business; we were children of sharecroppers, having worked together as a family in tobacco and picked cotton in Dover, North Carolina.

"Think and Grow Rich" by Napoleon Hill became my go-to book. Learning from attending workshops without hesitation became essential. We took the bull by the horns. Desperate to find out what would help our company name and brand get known quickly, mentors began to guide us. Let me share with you about this particular seminar.

Learning some of what we needed to know from 'Women in Business workshops, from someone who became my mentor, Rose Harper-Elder, from this panel of four women in business proved valuable.

Her goal was to discuss further the four steps she introduced. She said: Search for an experience that brought satisfaction; abstract a cause-and-effect model from what we saw in research;

create our own lesson plan and create a new program from what we learned; and finally, Ms. Elder said we should evaluate the method we have chosen.

Next was research from the Library of Congress which gave me a lesson in free publicity, which proves that any company can host a newsworthy special event to get 'free' publicity. I found that extremely interesting! Through the compilation of research on marketing and promotions by Vice-President Ernestine Grant, the media attention garnered by a small seafood business was remarkable. Ernestine was willing to research how to publicize a company and get great free publicity. For example, a seafood shop was seeking free publicity for their company on the map with a "crab race." It worked so well that the media attention catapulted the company to the public, such as .TV stations bragged about how their crab would win the race.

What could our company do to change the trajectory of where we were heading? Something exciting and newsworthy like the crab race, I thought. Suddenly, I had '*an aha*' moment. "*I know, why don't we commission an artist to sculpt a bronze bust of Reverend Jesse Louis Jackson? We can unveil the bust at our first Founder's Day event, which was February 11, 1984. The celebration of Critique's founders' day would be our first major event to promote the company.*" Not experienced in how to create a bronze bust. We all agreed, but the challenge was to figure out how to parlay the details and get a very busy and famous politician like Rev. Jesse Louis Jackson into a newsworthy media event. He deserved this honor, being the first Black man to complete a successful bid for the office of President of the United States. We needed to know how to convince him to sit for an artist to mold his image into an eternal sculpture?"

I thought of the Ten Commandments, "It's better to give than to receive."

Moving Forward After The Loss

We agreed to give the sculpture of Rev. Jackson to the Office of the Mayor as a gift to the city, especially since Mayor Barry and Rev. Jackson were close friends. That ought to get us on the map!

Not sure where to begin; the Yellow Pages was first. I began by making a few telephone calls, leaving messages, when finally, I decided to look for sculptors who had an address in southeast D.C., the lower-income section of the city; they can't possibly charge as much as the other uptown sculptors. When the phone rang, my first return call came from my southeast sculptor, Mrs. Retha Walden Gambaro, a wonderful Creek Indian sculptor from Oklahoma. She grew up in Phoenix, Arizona, later relocating to Washington, DC, where she owned an art gallery near Capitol Hill.

Delighted with the idea of a bust of Rev. Jackson, she said, "The timing is good. Let me give you some suggestions on how you can pull this off, and host small fund-raisers, I will wait for my deposit. I have a good feeling about you girls."

She was guided by spirit too!

She required two meetings with the great Reverend.

"Well!" I thought, "Who does she think I am to arrange such a meeting with a famous man like Jesse Jackson?"

She asked me to schedule the first meeting with the Reverend asap for photographs and measurements. The second meeting would have to be face-to-face. Retha required a sitting with Reverend to pose for a short time for the final touches.

The 1st meeting took four months to confirm. I made dozens of telephone calls. I became friends with Reverend Jackson's assistant Sylvia.

One day, Sylvia said during a telephone conversation, "You can meet with Reverend Jackson today at 1:00 pm, and that's the only time he has for an undetermined amount of time."

Running, I phoned Retha to see if they could come quickly on such short notice. In record time, my sister Jakki and I met the others at the National Rainbow Coalition offices. Retha and her photographer measured and photographed Reverend Jackson as I sat and chatted with him. This was an unbelievable task accomplished. It felt surreal. Here I was, a sharecropper's daughter, sitting and chatting with an internationally known Civil Rights Leader and former Presidential Candidate!

In my dream, I saw my visit with the Reverend become a reality, including, my mother, and me. But when the call finally came, my youngest sister Jacqulyn was there.

Retha took out her tape measurement and measured Rev. Jackson from his head to his shoulders, taking copious notes.

The second meeting requested must be a face-to-face meeting at her Gallery on Capitol Hill, which took place in January, during the Inauguration Celebration of President Ronald Reagan. The temperature was below freezing, the streets were icy, and snow blanketed the Greater Washington Metropolitan Area. News reports read, "Most of the Inauguration Celebrations of President Ronald Reagan have been canceled due to ice, sleet, and snow, with the exception of the Swearing in Ceremony."

"Well," I thought, The Reverend Jesse Jackson was in town for these events with nothing to do and nowhere to go. I began to make calls. I called and called and called his office! After getting through and being put on hold for hours, I laid on the bathroom floor, holding the telephone to my ear.

The secretary finally returned to the phone and said, "Reverend Jackson was staring at the phone, wondering why you wouldn't hang up." She continued, "Reverend said she's persistent, isn't she?"

Then finally, he said, "Tell her I'm coming to the studio for the sitting."

Jumping with joy, I got on the telephone and called Mrs. Gambaro to let her know that Reverend Jackson was coming to her studio. My sisters and I parked in front of the Gambaro's gallery to wait for the Reverend. We saw a car pull up, filled with African American men we could see the Reverend.

Excited, I said, "I'm too embarrassed to go inside to meet the Reverend."

So, I drove the car into the alley and hid as we watched the men get out and go inside. We drove home having gotten the job done!!!

I felt that I had been extremely pushy by holding on to the phone and didn't care to have a face-to-face encounter with Rev. Jackson. Retha phoned us later to tell us about the visit and asked why we didn't come in. Looking back, we wish the visit had not happened that way, but obviously, it happened as it should. One of my favorite scriptures is Romans 8:23, "And we know that all things work together for good to them who love God, and who are the called, according to His purpose." It happened as it should.

UNVEILED

The bronze sculpture was to be the showcase of Critique Career Management Services' first Founders Day Celebration.

The hotel was engaged, invitations mailed, and city and federal government dignitaries invited. All preparations were made to highlight the commemoration of the founding of "Critique."

As the date for the Founders Day Celebration approached, Retha advised us that the bust could not possibly be finished in time for the February celebration. My first thought was panic and embarrassment. But reacting negatively was a waste of time and energy. Retha offered a suggestion to cast a wax mold that would be suitable for the publicized unveiling. Critique's Founders Day Celebration was an overwhelming success. Those in attendance accepted the 'wax mold' in lieu of the completed bronze sculpture. They never knew the difference and felt we had planned our event this way. The sculptured bust of Reverend Jesse Louis Jackson was unveiled at the Omni Shoreham Hotel during our luncheon by D.C. Mayor Marion Barry.

Rev. Jackson could not attend, though he came to town for the occasion. He became ill and was hospitalized with pneumonia at Howard University Hospital. His family came. His mother and his children Santita, Jonathan, Jusef, and Jesse Jackson Jr were in attendance. The program was a luncheon for 500 people, complete with a dressing for success fashion show.

The Grant Sisters got the publicity we desired and needed. Exactly one year later, at the Washington Convention Center, we, the sisters, unveiled the first "official" bronze bust of the Reverend Jesse Louis Jackson, Sr., held at the Washington Convention Center. This time, the bust was cast in bronze and was a masterpiece!

The bust was presented to the District of Columbia government as a gift from Critique Career Management Services, just as we had planned. Actor LeVar Burton, star of the movie "Roots," came to participate in the Black History Month and Founders Day Celebration. We had corporate sponsors, and Mid-Atlantic Coca-Cola Bottling Company donated and sponsored a long banner hanging above the dais.

The unveiling of the Bronze Bust of Reverend Jesse Louis Jackson didn't come off just as we had planned, but it was a big hit just the same. The print and wire news media were there for the unveiling. Critique got the publicity that it needed. This event began to generate interest in a new business venture as we became known as the "Grant Sisters" event planners, though we had not planned to become event planners.

The sculptured bust project taught me to "Never Give up on a Dream," the theme song of the company, sung by Rod Stewart. By faith, we, the sisters applied the success principles; we believed and were able to see ourselves achieving our goal. Remember, I said that I had seen myself meeting with Reverend Jackson several times; that's faith, that's the power of a positive mental attitude, it is persistence, determination, and it is what helped to make the dream of my sisters and me become a reality.

This reinvention helped me to rise to become director of the Georgia Avenue Foundation, sponsors of the Georgia Avenue Day Parade and Festival, which more than 100,000 folks attended. Thanks to Washington Informer Newspaper for allowing me to write the Religion Corner, now syndicated for the past 18 years,

As Project Director of a national monument, I was appointed by .C.D.C. Councilman Frank Smith for the African American Civil War Memorial, which pays tribute to 209,145 US M Colored Troops and 7,000 White Officers who fought in The American Civil War. The unveiling, led by me as event manager with 200 volunteers, was broadcast live on CNN and CSPAN and seen on 163 TV stations across the nation.

YOU Can Reinvent Yourself to Rise?

Reprogram Your Thinking!
You must have an inner knowing of why your goal is for you. Instant Action is essential, so begin now.

Establish a deadline to reach your goal. Write your statement and make it clear.

Read it twice daily. SEE, FEEL & BELIEVE you have your goal. Be very careful whom you choose to be your mentor(s) and eliminate negative associates.

Lyndia Grant Briggs
Email: lyndiagrant@gmail.com
Website: lyndiagrant.com

Lyndia Grant Briggs, sharecropper's daughter, born in Kinston, North Carolina, picked cotton, harvested tobacco, missed months of school, yet remained an honor student.

A sibling of a family of 9 children, preacher-parents relocated the family to D.C. in 1965. After graduation, she married, it lasted 17 years. She worked and started her family relocating to the Bay Area for a decade.

Lyndia moved the three children back to DC. Becoming an entrepreneur, as president of Critique Career Management Services, Inc., with family. Lyndia led Critique to the 'official' Bronze Bust Unveiling of Rev. Jesse L. Jackson.

She's an author; radio show host, syndicated newspaper columnist, speaker; appointed to Inaugural Committees from U.S. Presidents, DC Mayors, to DC Councilmembers, was appointed project director for the national African-American Civil War Memorial, unveiled 1998, Washington, DC.

Lyndia is a college Graduate of Trinity Washington University. She earned her Communication Degree, BA/2000 & Master's/2005.

CHAPTER 8
INTERVIEW WITH DR. ZINA PIERRE

President & CEO of Reyarp Strategies Group, LLC (RSG), and Pastor of Bethel Restoration Church.

Dr. Tucker: I would love to hear a little more about you and your current work.

Dr. Zina Pierre: Thank you for this opportunity to be with you. It's such an honor and a privilege. I started my career in television and then ended up in the Clinton Administration. My last role was a commissioned officer role, in which I got to keep the title that I never used, "The Honorable," for the rest of my life because it was sanctioned by Congress. I was a special assistant to the president of intergovernmental affairs. In that role, I was President Bill Clinton's liaison to mayors and county officials. Also, I wanted the black state legislators on my plate. So, from there, I just decided, after we ended our two terms, that I would start my own thing.

I ended up starting a firm called the Washington Linkage Group. We represented a number of city and county governments around the country and some corporate and nonprofit entities. But on the spiritual side, I've been in church all my life. I was the first woman licensed to preach in the history of my home church, the First Baptist Church of Annapolis. I ran for public office and shifted my business.

Dr. Tucker: Where do you feel that women have needed the most support?

Dr. Zina Pierre: Mental support is the area. I'm a licensed counselor. I do vicarious trauma counseling. Vicarious trauma doesn't necessarily hit you directly but indirectly. Many of us have seen abuse and neglect. Perhaps it was to our mothers, grandmothers, aunties, cousins, or friends. That trauma rides with us throughout our lives without us even recognizing it until there's a triggering moment.

Dr. Tucker: Has there ever been a point where you have had to reinvent? I always ask that question, and people say, well, which time do you want to talk about it? But tell us where you've had to reinvent and what that has looked like. What does reinvention look like for you?

Dr. Zina Pierre: Well, I've had to reinvent myself multiple times, as many of us do. I used to be on the executive board of the National Council of Women with Dr. Dorothy Irene Height. I would hear her often say that African-American women, may not always do what we want to do, but we do what we must do. That has stuck in my spirit and my mind, and in my heart. Victory is my only option. Failure is not an option for me, but being successful is my only option. I'm a single girl, and what drives me may not drive other women from that perspective. But at the end of the day, it's not just about me. The money that I make, it's for me to be a blessing to people too.

I often tell God to listen; in order for me to be a blessing, I need a blessing. When I was leaving the Clinton White House, Dr. Height asked me a question.

Dr. Height said, "Miss Pierre, what are you going to do with yourself after leaving the White House?"

I said, "Well, Dr. Height, I really desire to put my hat out there and lobby. I've made all of these relationships here in the White House. I took care of a lot of people and opened doors for a lot of people. I built the relationships. So let me just try my hand at it."

She said, "Well, come and work in the building. I'll give you office space. You don't have to worry about paying for anything. Just come in and continue to help me do the work that I'm doing."

There were times when I wrote her speeches and did the research for her. My firm was getting resources. We were going after funding to support some of the things she was doing in the building, so we didn't take a dime from her. It was a great relationship where we had an opportunity to have an office on Pennsylvania Avenue. I went from 1600 Pennsylvania Avenue to 700 Pennsylvania Avenue. We were literally right in between the US Capitol and the White House.

It was really a corridor of power because Dr. Height knew so many presidents. She counseled so many presidents. The White House frequently called on her for her opinion on different things. So, I had never done this before. I have no mentors to show me how to do this. I just walked in that thing blindly. I built relationships, and the people I cared for, came back, and remembered me, and doors were opened. Most of my contracts were relationship contracts because I had established strong relationships with different mayors and county officials. I didn't get the contracts because of just that. I did the work, and I worked really hard.

There were big firms with 200 lawyers or more, and here I was with just me and two lobbyists I'd hired that started as junior lobbyists and an assistant. I was the only African-American female-owned federal lobbying firm in the country, well, one of less than four. There are plenty of African-American lobbyists, who were working for corporations, companies, and organizations. I was working for myself. I represented Baltimore City, the City of Denver Health Department, Prince George's County, and Anne Arundel County. I mean, at one point, I had four major jurisdictions right in Maryland.

God opened a lot of major doors. Unions like AFSCME and International Union was a client, and Launa was a client. DC government agencies were clients. As time shifted, we went into a federal moratorium when President Obama came in. There was a moratorium placed on earmarks and appropriations, which was what I did as a specialty. When all of those went out, so did all of my clients because I could not help them find funding. I was a public interest lobbyist. So, I was helping people find more resources for their CDCs and helping the county get resources for a mobile dental van after the young boy died from an infection in his mouth due to a decayed tooth.

We worked on the radio inoperability situation when 911 hit. There was no radio capability or connection between DC and Maryland, and they needed new cell towers and equipment to be able to do that. My firm worked tirelessly to get resources to address that inoperability. Then, the resources started drifting, and I found myself having to close down shop because I couldn't sustain the folk anymore.

Reinvention means t you have to reinvest in yourself, but you will also go through a crazy walking period of faith. So instead of paying myself anything, I paid the staff because I knew that it was going to be hard for them to find jobs. I lost my home because I neglected myself to take care of my staff. Finally, I just said, okay, I got to shut this down and just reinvent myself. I shut it down and reestablished another company in 2016, and God provided, and he still continues to provide. So, I went from heavy lobbying in the federal sector to doing training and development.

Now. I do executive coaching. I do personality assessments and build diversity, equity, and inclusion frameworks for organizations or government agencies to help people figure out how to create a true culture of inclusion and belonging. A lot of people don't think about this the right way. When you mention diversity, equity, and inclusion, people say, I'm not a racist. I have black friends. It's not about race; it's about equity. Yes, equity has played a part in race, but there have been times when we have been inequitable to ourselves. So, this was about training and teaching people about understanding what biases are.

That whole reinvention piece is real. Because in the midst of me reinventing myself in my business, I was reinventing myself in ministry. I launched a church, and I was like, God. I started the new company in 2016. I started the church in 2018 and lost my house in 2018. A lot was going on. All I had was my faith. It was my faith and my patience with myself that allowed me to understand what reinvention really was at a time when I was in so much pain and felt like, wow, God, I've blessed all these people over the years. I've served, and I've done what you told me to do; how did I end up in this place? But God always has a plan that we don't necessarily understand, nor should we. But he had a major plan, and he gave me double for my trouble and all the stuff I was dealing with.

Dr. Tucker: And he always does that. He'll always do that.

Dr. Zina Pierre: Yes, he will.

Dr. Tucker: Wow. So, you just gave us so much, such a story of reinvention there. I mean, something that definitely, I know that women who read this will pull out some things they can use if they desire to reinvent, for sure. What specific tips may you have for women who are looking to make a change, who may be a little afraid but who know that they are up to do something meaningful and different if they want better? What tools do you say they need to have?

Dr. Zina Pierre: Well, some of the tips that women can use as we look at this whole thing of reinvention is that you've got to walk by faith and not by sight, that you're in a season of reinvestment. What you will not invest in, you can't reinvent, or you can't invent. So that means I got to take time to hear from God. That's the hardest thing for a busy person to do. It's the hardest thing. But you got to get to a place where you settle in so you can hear the download in your spirit. After all, God will give you witty inventions and ideas if you just and sit still. So, my first point is that you got to settle in and take time with yourself. Don't feel guilty about taking time for yourself.

People will make you feel so guilty when you choose to pull back so that you can hear from God and hear yourself speak. Once you settle in, you got to face what's facing you. Look at the picture of what you see here and deal with it. The problem is, it's easier for us to put our heads in the sand and shut down and just hope it goes away and everything will be lovely in a few days.

It might be a Cinderella story, but it's not our reality. Facing what's facing you gives you a real perspective of what you see in the natural so that you know what to pray for in the spirit realm. For example, if I can see Zina doesn't have confidence, I will go find every scripture on confidence. I will pray those scriptures until that confidence becomes confident. Sometimes you're going to see stuff that you don't like. You're going to see the little girl that's afraid, and you're going to see the little girl that was hurt. You're going to see the little girl who was told she would never be anything.

You're going to see the little girl that was told she could be everything. So, you're going to see all these different angles about you, and the best thing to do is own up to it, whatever it is, and write these things down. Whatever you want God to remove, tell him to remove it. But you have to agree with it. What does that mean? Don't open the front door or don't close the front door but keep the back door open. You have to make a decision. Decide if you'll close some doors that you know are distracting you.

Secondly, once you face what's facing you, you have to walk in this place of faith. I can only tell you the life that I live. I walk by faith, and sometimes I do by sight too. Let's just be real talk, facing what's facing you. Sometimes that faith walk is not easy because you've seen enough, been through enough, come out of enough, and gone into enough. You're just over it! You're tired. This is when you get to walk in this place of faith because faith cancels out fear.

Third, you got to be focused. Once you get to facing what's facing you, you must get to that place of faith. You say, God, I know the bills are heavy right now, but I know you can. Ask God to send you divine helpers. People who lift you up, not just hold your hand, but lift you up. We got enough hand holders. Holding my hand does not carry me to the next place. But when you lift me up, I can see things in a different light. The focus is so key because when you are in that place of reinvention, you have to be laser-focused, or you will fall off the plan. God will say one thing, and you will think He's saying another because you're not focused; you're scattered and all over the place.

Lastly, follow through. Everything I was focused on, I followed through on it. I promise you; I haven't always been that girl. The follow-through was my biggest crutch or situation that hurt me the most because there were doors open, but I just didn't follow through with them, whether it was because I didn't trust them, or I was too busy. So, I say to you, don't let your busy be so busy that you end up broke.

Dr. Tucker: Now that›s powerful right there. Don›t let your busy be so busy that you end up broke. And it›s so easy to do that. Not giving our best. Yes. But just giving that.

Dr. Zina Pierre: One more thing. I was praying one day to the Lord because I was frustrated, and I said, God, why is it that I can't get to that millionaire status that I once was in? What am I not doing right? I'm doing the same things that I did before. He said, Zina, you have become stale. I said, what do you mean by that, God? He said I expired some of those things that I gave you 20 years ago or ten years ago. Those things have expired, but you are trying to resuscitate what I have already taken off your plate. Sometimes we try to resuscitate dead things that have ended, and he wants you to come up with something new. All he wants you to do is sit still, face what's facing you, and walk by faith and not by sight.

Dr. Tucker: Thank you so, so much for being here. Again, I greatly appreciate you taking some time and chiseling out some time to talk to us about this topic.

Dr. Zina Pierre: Thank you.

To reinvent is to be reborn. For many it's the shedding of old hurts and pains in order to allow the beauty beneath to see the light of day. So many of these stories wreak with vitality, hope and promise.

Here you will hear the recollection of events that caused hearts to stop as they happened, and still bring about feelings of suffocation as they're retold. So many opportunities to give up. Many times it seemed so much easier to turn around and go back. There was safety in what was left behind. Circumstances remained stagnant and painful, but safety often seemed to be a nice trade-off for the future's unknown. These chapters give a glimpse into the lives of women who had to endure indescribable physical and mental pain. They survived, and they've lived to tell about it.

How beautiful it is to hear about the barriers that were broken and the lives that were reshaped. These women did whatever was necessary. They were courageous and innovative, demonstrating a pioneering spirit and determination to achieve something unprecedented. Their successes became benchmarks that motivated many others, paving the way for future progress.

They all took a chance on reinvention. They give us hope, and their paths provide a template for new possibilities.

Every morning we get a chance to be different. A chance to change. A chance to be better. Your past is your past. Leave it there. Get on with the future part, honey.

Simone de Beauvoir

Pixie Lee

CHAPTER 9
REINVENTED WITH DIVINE INTERVENTION

Being a business owner and entrepreneur can entail learning some difficult lessons. I'm still learning those lessons. In the first edition of Reinvented to Rise, I talked about how I became a life coach. It was never on my radar, honestly, when I first heard the word, I didn't even know what one was. After completing my certification, I didn't want to build my business the traditional way. I did that the first time with my accounting firm, so this time, I said, first I would write my book. Fast forward five years, and here I am a serial entrepreneur with several businesses still reinventing herself on what seems like a regular basis.

I'm sure you're wondering how I got to that point that a reinvention is necessary more than once. Well, I'm glad you asked. Being in business is not an easy task. There are several lessons that you can't learn until you're actually in it. You can definitely get the guidance and assistance you need, but some stuff is on-the-job training.

Let's start where we left off the last time. I am Pixie Lee, Content Creator Extraordinaire. I ghostwrite for you when you don't know what to say or how to say it. I'm the coach who tells you what you need to hear in order to get you moving in the right direction. I'm the speaker who motivates you from the stage in person and the virtual stage to know it's your job to walk in purpose. I'm the author who writes books that help you heal from the inside out. Seems simple enough, right? WRONG! The first lesson I had to learn was that you would be forever reinventing yourself and your business. Since the last book, I've started two additional businesses to go along with the businesses I already had. I'm sure you're asking why? Because expanding my business and niching down to a specific audience was a must. See, I learned the hard way that you can't serve everyone, and everybody isn't your client. You must have a specific audience that you are targeting. I know many people think this will limit your income and potential client pool, but it's just the opposite. Niching down will give you a wide pool of potential clients. And although you've niched down, it doesn't mean that you can't take business from those who are not in your niche.

Let me make it plain. Because I am a Content Creator who focuses on writing and all the words, I started a publishing company. During the pandemic, I started seeing people who were depressed and giving up because of how the world was moving. There was death all around us. Watching television was only making matters worse. I wanted to be able to change the narrative. I know from experience that you have to be careful what you watch, listen to, and read because what you put in is exactly what you would push out. With that in mind, I decided it was time for God's people to hear from the people God had called. I started PL Publishing, and the first person I needed was my father, Rev. R.L. Glover.

My dad has been preaching for over 50 years. He started at the age of 13. I've always heard everyone tell him he needed to write a book. Thankfully he agreed. After we selected the ministers who would join him and the message to the reader, PL Publishing published its first collaboration, An Anchor for the Ages. Now let me connect these dots. Although I started another company, I'm still in the same niche I was in before writing and words.

And now I've added a new layer and title to my identity. But that's also when the trouble started brewing. If you're not sure, let me confirm for you now. Once you are walking in your calling or purpose, there will always be trouble brewing. I knew it in the back of my mind, but whew, chile, when it rains, it pours.

I'm sure you've heard people who say the devil is busy. Well, as I told you before, all the pieces of your puzzle will always fit together. The good and the bad will always work together for your good. Meaning everything that happens isn't from the devil. Sometimes God sends situations and allows situations to occur in order to stretch and mold you into where he needs you to be and go where you are saying you want to go. With that being said, in June, I had health challenges again. This time I was off work for six weeks and during that six-week time, my mother received her breast cancer diagnosis. To say my life was turned upside-down is putting it lightly. Everything flashed before my eyes. I couldn't concentrate on my healing because now I was worried about my mom. As we walked this journey, I often would sit down to work my business, and I would think to myself, what is even the point?

God had to work on me, my mindset, and my attitude in order to get me together. While on this journey, I finally found my footing, and another boulder was slung at my head. My daughter was pregnant and ended up in the hospital. Her pregnancy was labeled high risk, and we faced some serious decisions during the last three months of her pregnancy. I sat in the hospital that day and cried my eyes out. I couldn't even begin to understand anything that was going on. I had given birth to three healthy children, and I felt like I was pregnant for the first time again, trying to understand what the doctor was saying. I felt like I was strong enough to handle anything that came my way, but within the last 365 days, I found out quickly that I wasn't as ready and equipped as I thought I was. I was shaken. I was scared. And I was worried.

Let's fast forward to the summertime. My mom is on her maintenance treatment, and my daughter delivered a healthy baby boy, and she is back to 100%. Things were looking up in my personal life, but my business had taken a hit because I wasn't fully focused and doing what I needed to do. Things kept going from bad to worse. The clients I was attracting weren't doing the things I needed them to do to accomplish their goals. I had clients who were paying sporadically or when they wanted to and thought that was good enough for me to work around the clock without compensation. Then I had clients that wanted and requested services they hadn't paid for at all. Again, when it rains, it pours. Things were moving along but not in the direction I wanted them to. I was getting traction but not the traction I needed or wanted. I was at the point where I was contemplating my next step.

I mean, think about it. I've already done all the work to build my business without all this drama. I was successful but not at the level I thought I should be. I wasn't necessarily comparing myself to anyone, and I certainly wasn't jealous of their success. You never know someone's story and sacrifices in order to get what they have, so that didn't bother me. I always wondered; do I make a difference? Am I really reaching the right people? I even asked myself why am I doing this? It became so much that I thought about shutting everything down and walking away. Maybe this isn't for me. Maybe the impact I'm leaving isn't what I think it is. Where did I go wrong?

Here are all these questions that require answers. And I had no answers. I sat and sat and sat. At one point, it became depressing. I literally walked away from everything, and no one knew it. I hid behind the mask that everything was ok and kept it pushing, knowing deep inside that I was one post away from saying goodbye on social media. I never said anything to anyone, and one Sunday at church, daddy preached a message about the miracle of going through. God always gives us vision with the provision and the divine intervention where the Master steps in. That struck a chord with me. Instantly, that got my attention. I knew that message was just for me. Listening to that sermon, gave me exactly what I needed in order to stand up, reinvent myself and my company this time and keep going. What I took away from that sermon were lessons that I learned for reinvention, and I believe they will serve you well if you have come to the point where a reinvention is necessary. First, don't give up. That day I realized that. I can't give up before my miracle happens, and God is the difference-maker that I need. While I know that God is the center of my life and my businesses, I clearly need to go back to the drawing board. No situation stays the same after the divine intervention takes place. I felt that all in my spirit. I have always known that giving up wasn't an option, but it was a different, I can't give up this time.

Secondly, decide how you want your reinvented situation to look. I went home and took out a piece of paper, and it was time to get my master plan for 2023. Yes, all of this just happened in the last six months. I had to sit down and think about what I wanted my companies and myself to look like in the upcoming year. I had to figure out what didn't work in 2022 and the past and change that for the future. I have two companies that work hand in hand. I needed to make sure people knew those were two separate companies. The last company is a TV show network, and I'm creating a tv show based on the first company. I needed to make sure that company and tv show stood by themselves but also worked hand in hand, with the mother ship and my publishing company. It's vitally important to make sure that you are returning to the drawing board every year. You have to take a really close look at the achievements and the wins and the lessons in order to see where you have room for improvement. I never count them as losses because I can always find something in there that was a win, even if it wasn't a complete win.

Let me pull it all together for you. The definition of reinventing is to change something so much that it appears entirely different. The third lesson I learned was huge! There will be more reinventions as you move forward. It's not a one-and-done. It's perfectly fine to start over multiple times, especially if you're like me and have had to do so. You have to figure out what is working and what is not. Where do you need to pivot? What should you remove? I sat down and looked at each company individually. I know exactly who my niche is for all of the companies. I also had to reinvent myself.

My final lesson directly speaks to who you are. . In the world of business, we often achieve great things. However, when people ask us to describe ourselves, we tend to downplay our accomplishments, afraid of sounding too confident or conceited. But I want to share some advice with you; you should never diminish your achievements. You don't have to sit down, blend in and stay in the background to make anyone else feel comfortable. If someone asks who you are, say it with air in your chest and attitude in your voice. I had to realize I am an accomplished 7-time author. I am an accomplished publisher. I am a motivational speaker and a successful business coach! Those are not goals I want to accomplish; those are goals I have achieved. I had to change my mindset and respect myself in order for others to see me and my accomplishments and respect them too. When I say put some respect on my name, it's because I've earned it, and I know it.

To succeed, you must be willing to pivot and reinvent yourself. You cannot avoid reinvention; it is essential. Giving up is not a viable option. Winning is the only path to take.

Surround yourselves with people who have the same mentality that you have. Look at every day as the day you level up because staying the same isn't an option either.

Pixie Lee
Contact: pixielee@bizzybossymommy.com
Instagram: @bizzybossymommy

She hails from the big A, Atlanta, GA. She was educated in the Cobb County Schools system and went on to get her Accounting degree at Chattahoochee Tech. After years of running a successful Accounting firm, she returned to Corporate America. After being laid off, she received her certification as a Life Coach. She is the author of The Power of Purpose and Forgiveness is Key.

During the pandemic, she started her publishing company, PL Publishing. She helps men and women in ministry write the right book to tell their stories. She also entered into a partnership to form the KDCP Network. This network is geared towards women in business doing business together.

In her spare time, she spends time with her family especially her 2 daughters, son, and her grandson.

Pixie believes and lives by the mantra, if she takes care of God's people, God will take care of her.

Dr. Deidra W. Hill

CHAPTER 10

MORNING CAME, AND I WAS STILL ALIVE

The scars above and below my left eye used to be painful reminders of the tragedy I had endured. Now, they are triumphant badges of courage and survival. From my arms and legs to my torso, lacerations cover me. I could have had the scars removed at any time during my many surgeries, but I chose not to.

"They'll heal in time," my grandmother said. "Just use a little cocoa butter."

Today, the indelible marks are not as pronounced as they used to be, having faded somewhat over time. Yet, I gaze upon them occasionally, tracing over with my fingers and remembering that surviving this means I can survive anything.

In early May 1986, in Santee, South Carolina, three college students were killed one week before graduation. The students had attended South Carolina State College, where Dr. M. Maceo Nance was president. Many great achievements occurred during his administration, and the campus grew exponentially. President Nance began his term during a turbulent time in 1968 when three students were massacred for trying to integrate a bowling alley in Orangeburg. Uncannily, he would end his term 18 years later as he began his presidency—with the death of

Morning Came, And I Was Still Alive

three students. While much has been written and extolled about those who died, my story is about survival.

I have told this story many times, but this is the first time I have ever written about it to share with others. I hope readers will gain strength, courage, and perseverance to overcome challenges in their lives. I also want readers to find meaning and purpose beyond the day-to-day activities that can consume us and cause complacency.

I was a senior at SC State, majoring in English. My classmates and I were ready to celebrate after finishing all the requirements for the baccalaureate degree program. The annual Greek Picnic in Santee State Park was as much a year-end celebration as it was a rite of passage for seniors.

Students donned Greek paraphernalia representing their sorority and fraternity. Greek life on an HBCU campus is extraordinary, and the Greek picnic was not an event to miss. With a friend visiting from out of town, I had planned to drive my car. However, two of my specs (pronounced SPESH; short for special and pertaining to a favorite recently initiated soror) approached us and offered us a ride. So, we hopped in the back seat and rode with them.

The weather was beautiful, warm, and clear. When we arrived, there was the usual camaraderie, music, and food representative of a southern-style cookout. We did not stay long, and as expected, people dropped in and out throughout the day.

Leaving the park is a blur to me. I cannot recall how long we were in the car before suddenly things went dark. From this point on, I do not remember what happened until I awoke in the intensive care unit at Orangeburg-Calhoun Regional Hospital several hours later. The details of the impact on a Santee highway and my arrival in ICU were recounted to me.

Another car full of students traveling on the opposite side of the highway crossed the median and hit our car head-on. My sorors in the front seats died instantly.

My friend beside me in the back seat said that my body looked twisted like a pretzel. He said I kept repeatedly saying, "I can't breathe."

Later, I learned that my lungs had collapsed. He got out of the car but quickly fell to the ground, not realizing that his leg had been shattered. We both were suffering from shock trauma.

One of the students in the other car had been thrown from the vehicle and died on impact. The back passenger door on my side behind the driver of the car was unrecognizable, looking like silver scrap metal. I needed to be cut out of the vehicle. After my seemingly lifeless body was retrieved from the car, they rushed me to the hospital.

The architect of sanity during the melee of my ICU intake was my best friend, Tracy Wright. As one of the first to arrive at the hospital, she became the point person for my care and well-being, as my parents were hundreds of miles away in Maryland. My brother was four hours away in Atlanta attending college, and my closest relative, my aunt Dr. Adelle Stewart, a microbiology professor, and researcher at SC State, was too hysterical to assist doctors. Tracy answered doctors' questions, consented to my surgery, determined who could see me in ICU, and gave my parents the comfort they needed while they traveled to Orangeburg.

Doctors emphasized that my parents come right away if they wanted any chance of spending time with me, as I was not expected to survive the night. The extent of my injuries was too severe, such as chest and abdominal injuries, multiple fractures to legs and arms, and numerous lacerations. Morning came, and I was still alive.

Road to Recovery

The road to recovery is long and littered with setbacks. It is disappointingly slow, and with each step forward, there seem to be several steps backward. I have learned that no matter how bad things seem, it could be worse. I look for glimmers of light, small signs of progress that are difficult to see at first but pack a powerful punch when repeated. Recovery teaches you what you are made of; for me, it was a test of courage and perseverance.

While in ICU, I had been intubated, and my right hand was partially restrained to prevent me from pulling out the tube that was helping to keep me alive. My left hand was of no threat as it was paralyzed and unusable. Unable to speak, I was given a writing pad and pen, which I used to write down questions about my care and progress. Despite my injuries, I was unusually optimistic about recovery. I did not realize then that the journey to walking again would take almost two years.

Still, I felt early on that everything was going to be okay. What scared me most at the time was looking at all the sad faces of people who visited me in the ICU. I remember wondering what I must look like for people to be so sad and aghast when they saw me. For several weeks, I was a sore sight to watch as wounds turned to scabs, and scabs fell off, leaving keloids and dark splotches.

One week passed, and I was still in ICU. It was Commencement Day at SC State. Since I could not participate in the ceremony, my mother was allowed to walk across the stage on my behalf to receive the undergraduate diploma for the Bachelor of Arts degree in English from President Nance. The university also recorded the ceremony and provided a CD, which to this day, I have never watched. After what I had been through and with recovery as the main focus, commencement seemed minuscule.

After another week passed, my condition was upgraded to stable, and I was eventually moved to a private hospital room. The journey to learning how to walk again began with the extremely uncomfortable and now outdated process of traction so that my bones stayed in place and healed properly. Traction is almost unbearable as you cannot move around comfortably in the hospital bed. My left leg was hoisted in the air, while a metal rod had been placed into my right femur to keep it secure.

I was surrounded by family and friends, especially my paternal grandmother, affectionately known as the Chief. Sitting with me daily in the hospital room, she was quiet and stoic, full of wise sayings, and a strong and faithful woman who always prayed. I never saw tears, worry, or fear in her eyes. I saw that everything was going to be all right.

Chief was the one who told me not to worry about the scars; "They'll heal in time."

Finally, I was ready to leave Orangeburg for my home in Maryland. I had moved from traction to a wheelchair. While friends were celebrating a graduation, starting their careers, preparing for graduate school, or planning weddings, my dreams changed. I looked forward to sleeping in my own room, using the bathroom, walking, and regaining independence and mobility.

I felt frustrated and upset, especially when I started physical and occupational therapy. The pace was so slow, dragging on for months, and it seemed as if there was no progress. I became flippant with the health care providers because I did not see the point of wasting time with exercises if I could not see evidence that they were working.

The nerve damage to my left arm rendered my wrist, hand, and fingers motionless. There were days when I did not have the energy to exercise, but I did it nonetheless. Then one day, out of nowhere, there was a slight quiver in my fingers. On another day, my wrist moved. While I still could not hold my left hand up for long without the assistance of my right hand, I could move it. That was all the evidence I needed. From then on, I worked out with fierce determination. I would regain at least 90 percent usage in my left hand and fingers.

My leg was healing in a lighter, more manageable cast. Still, my only form of movement was by wheelchair. By late summer, I had graduated to a walker, which I did not use for long. I wanted to walk with crutches, and by fall, my wish was granted. In fact, it was important to me to attend Homecoming, and I did. That was the first time many classmates had seen me since ICU, so I wanted to assure people that I was well. But I still had a long way to go. I could not stand for long, and my legs needed elevation to prevent swelling.

My orthopedic doctor promised that if I continued to progress well, he would have the cast removed by Christmas. In the days leading to the holiday, I anticipated my doctor's appointment with glee. The customary X-rays were conducted, as I waited for the cast removal. When he returned to the exam room, the expression on his face revealed the bad news. The bone in my left leg was not healing correctly and was crooked. It would need to be broken and reset, which meant another surgery.

I would be in a cast, albeit a new one, for several more weeks, months. I was starting to feel the strain of mental and emotional stress and questioned whether I would ever walk again. So, I focused on occupational therapy—how to do things for myself such as eating, bathing, using the bathroom, going up and down stairs, standing up and sitting down, and getting in and out of a car.

By spring, almost a year later, the cast was finally removed. Even though I would continue to use two crutches for a while, I felt so free. My physical therapy continued for several months. Two crutches became one crutch, and one crutch became none. By the time I started graduate school in fall of 1987, I was walking on my own. During a follow-up visit to my doctor, he asked why I was limping. According to the latest X-rays he had taken, he said there was no medical reason for me to be limping and that it was in my head. With back straight, shoulders upright, and chin up, I walked out of his office that day for the last time and with no limp.

Blueprint for Survival

Surviving a head-on collision in which three people died was the first tragedy of my life, but it would not be the last. This experience is so pivotal because I have used the lessons learned to overcome later tragedies. Recurring themes of faith, family, perseverance, courage, and purpose are critical elements on the journey toward healing. After 37 years, the blueprint is still working.

Believe in a power greater than your own. Surviving the unimaginable when three others lost their lives, surviving when doctors did not expect me to pull through, and surviving when the idea of survival was not an option are what I tightly grasped.

Despite frustration and setbacks, I knew that faith, instinctive and not by rote, would pull me through.

Lean into family and friends for support. This is not charity; it is life. For those who want to help, let them help. Some people do not have to ask what you need because they intuitively know and will do what is needed. Others want to help but do not know how and may need guidance. Prepare a list of ways people can help and share it with family and friends. I enjoyed having people sit with me, massage my legs and feet, especially after physical therapy, and drive me places and wheel me around.

Patience is invaluable and should be honed. Without patience, I would not have endured the re-breaking and resetting of my leg and starting the process over again. Healing, whether physical, mental, or emotional, takes time. Avoid defining time. Take the time to heal without setting an actual timeline. You will know when to move on as well as when not to tarry too long. Patience is needed in order to persevere.

Accept that your life will be forever changed. Reinvention is building again what did not exist before. After the tragic experience, I was no longer the same person. I started to see life very differently. Small things that may have irritated me before no longer took hold. I found chitchat useless. Addressing issues that affected people's lives was more important.

Rediscovering who I am and defining my purpose was essential. Whatever I chose to do had to have meaning. I was given another chance at life, and it was important to use it to help others who may be facing insurmountable challenges. After dabbling in healthcare and nonprofit fields, I finally found my footing in higher education, where I have sojourned for 25 years, partnering with colleges and universities to tell stories that impact students' lives, communities, and the world.

I think back on May 1986 often, and it is simply amazing what I have overcome. While this was the first tragedy I had ever experienced, I found the strength and courage to face a string of others.

I would later graduate from American University with a Master of Arts degree in journalism and public affairs just two years after the accident. It was the first time I walked across the stage for a college degree, and it was not my last. The morning continues to come, and I remain alive and well.

Dr. Deidra W. Hill
Contact: deidra@dwhillassociates.com

Dr. Deidra W. Hill has been leading communications and marketing programs for higher education institutions for 25 years. Her work has been recognized by the National Council for Marketing and Public Relations Paragon and Medallion Awards, Public Relations Society of America Best in Maryland, and CASE Accolades awards. She launched D.W. Hill & Associates, Inc., to create and implement solutions for organizations struggling with their most critical communications challenges. She earned a Doctor of Education degree from Morgan State University, master's degree in journalism and public affairs from American University, and a bachelor's in English from South Carolina State University.

CHAPTER 11

INTERVIEW WITH JUDGE WANDA KEYES HEARD

(Retired) Chief Judge, 8th Judicial Circuit of Maryland, Baltimore City

Dr. Tucker: Judge Heard, thank you so much for being with us today.

Judge Heard: I'm honored to be here and have the opportunity to share.

Dr. Tucker: Can you tell us a little about yourself and what you're currently doing?

Judge Heard: I practiced law for 40 years. The first 17, I was a litigator for most of that time as a prosecutor. I spent a small amount of time doing civil defense and criminal defense work. In 1999, I was appointed to the bench, which is the circuit court for Baltimore City. I served for 21 years until I retired in December 2019. As a result of my tenure there, I became the chief judge of that court; this was an honor for me. It was also a historic honor because no woman had ever served as the chief judge of that court.

Now I'm retired. I kicked my shoes off and took off my robe, and decided I would sit.

Dr. Tucker: I think I already know part of the answer to this question. What is it that you're really passionate about?

Judge Heard: Well, I think that one of the influences that I provide to the youth in our community, especially in Baltimore, is to represent an alternative to what they may see on the street corner. I looked around at my colleagues, and most of them were associating with each other. They were involved in judicial committees or conferences or seminars, or they were on legal committees or projects or the Bar Association. But as I traveled around the schools and grassroots community organizations that mentor kids, I didn't see a lot of my colleagues. I would try my best to draw them in and encourage them to spend some of their time with the youth. I would say, "I know you have a family, and I know you have kids, but take some of your time and devote it to the community."

When I see my grandbaby, I think of promise. Jokingly, I had a conversation with her about the election of 2060 and how she was going to run for president. The sky is the limit. When we were kids, they said we could be anything. But it wasn't until 2022 that I saw a black woman sworn into the Supreme Court of the United States.

Dr. Tucker: Your entire life has truly been one of perseverance. You're a true history-maker. You've endured many trials along the way, and I just want to know from you, what is it that you feel was the cost of getting to where you are? What were some of the sacrifices you had to make in order to get to where you are?

Judge Heard: Well, first, I have to say that when I told my parents I wanted to be a lawyer, I was about 9 or 10. I was a Perry Mason kid. He always got the bad guy to admit guilt while on the witness stand. I thought it was amazing. He walked around with this big legal book called The Corpus Juris. It was all about truth and justice in the American way. I bought into that hook, line, and sinker. I also bought into the idea that I could have it all. My father encouraged me to go into a field where there weren't people that looked like me.

It was a predominantly white male lawyer that I would see. He was encouraging me and saying, your gender, your race, don't matter. You can be whatever you want to be with education. My mother was a nurse. She had a career and a family that she was raising. My dad was a teacher, and then he became an administrator. So the message was, you can have it all. I turned on the television, and there's Gloria Steinem, and she's saying, ladies, you can have it at all. So I bought into, I'm going to have it all. I'm going to have a career, and I'm going to have a family; I'm going to have it all wasn't true. Some sacrifices made back then often caused women to choose between having a family and having a career.

If they pressed, you were ostracized occasionally because you weren't a good mother if you weren't staying home with your children. Aren't you neglecting your family if you are in the workplace? Oh, by the way, I'm not going to start an hour or two later so you can take your kid to the doctor because your child has a 104 temperature. You need to make a choice. What is it going to be? Are you going to be a lawyer or a litigator, or are you going to be a wife and a mother?

You can't have both, and no, I won't call you by your hyphenated name. Pick which name you want. You can't have it hyphenated. I mean, it was a story that was fed to me that I bought, but I quickly saw the choices I would have to make. Now things have changed. Back when I started, we didn't have state-ordered maternity or parental leave. It wasn't acceptable to bring your children to the office. I mean, work from home; you got to be kidding me. We didn't have all of that. Remember, we were still using payphones.

Consider the women who were coming through during the women's movement, and the civil rights movement, who wanted to have everything that was being offered to others. Wanted to have a career and have a family and be accepted for the quality of the work they did every day, not on whether or not they were married. For fear you're going to get pregnant and leave, the firm is afraid to hire you. We believe you will get pregnant and leave to raise your family.

Enter Wanda. I get pregnant. I'm in a big law firm, and I say, "Oh, no, I'm going to work. I'm going to have this baby. I'm going to work right up to when the baby's born, and then after the baby's born, I'm going to make arrangements for childcare, and I'm coming back to work."

That was not something that was expected of me. There are far too many items for me to run down the sacrifices that had to be made. But sacrifices, they were deep.

I am happy that those scars are now healing. But I'm even happier that the community and society have changed in such a way that women in the workplace are more acceptable and that provisions have been made for women to work and have a family. More importantly, it is more acceptable for men to take off time to be present in the lives of their children and their families. So those are a few of the sacrifices. But I mean, I only talked about from a gender perspective, I didn't even get into as an African American woman, walking in the room and being the only woman in the room. Only African American in the room. Now, as my ex-husband told me one day, and it was your meeting too. Did you notice that you were running a meeting and you were the only woman in the room? You and I were the only African Americans in the room, and everyone else was white males? If I focused on my race and my gender every time I started a meeting, I'd never get anything done. So, you work hard, and you establish yourself. And in instances like that, sometimes the establishment means you sacrifice to be the best that you're able to be and force them to come to you even when they really don't want to.

Dr. Tucker: When they don't want to. Oh, my goodness. Wow! The sacrifices were vast. I know that what you've given is truly just the top of the crust, so to speak. Definitely not all of them. We're talking reinvention. That's what this whole project is about. I hear reinvention throughout this entire story. Did it really take some reinventing to get the things that you needed to get done? Those sacrifices sound like there was a whole lot of reinventing going on in there.

Judge Heard: It's funny you used the word reinvention because when we talked earlier, I had to think about what you meant by reinvention. My father considered me a locomotive on a locomotive track. He said, you had a goal, and you headed for it. You never went off on one side or took a shortcut on the other. You just headed down the road. What I passed to stay on the track is how I view my life. I don't see myself going off on a side road and then reinventing myself to come back. I see myself as always in the same place, headed in the same direction.

As I went along, there were things that I missed out on. I always wanted to have a loving family relationship. I never expected to be divorced. I never expected to be a single parent. Did I reinvent myself? Yeah. Because I went from being married to being a single parent, and my career stayed on track. I just had to figure out how to be on that track as a single parent. How do you get to court when you have a child with 104 temperature, and you have to take her to the doctor? How do you do that? On the track, you find a backup, you find helpers. You hire people to care for your child when you can't be present. You don't want a latchkey child. That means you'll have to find someone to pick her up at the end of the day to stay with her until you're able to be there. I had a bed roll under my desk when I was in the US attorney's office because when I would have the nighttime duty, there was no one at two or three o'clock in the morning to take Whitney.

I had to take her with me, but she's sleeping. So the bedroll had all sorts of treats, toys, a flashlight, and things for her to play with under my desk while I talked to the agent about the search and seizure warrant that he had to do at two o'clock in the morning or whatever. Do you want to call that reinvention? Well, that's the single parent. I can't leave this six-year-old home alone. I have to take her with me. So I found ways to stay on track and remain true to my profession. In one of my marriages, my husband received a promotion, and went to the West Coast, and I was on the East Coast. In order to follow him, I would have to leave the job where I was one of, I think, six or eight African-American women in positions of power in the US Attorney's office nationally.

So, it didn't; there was no going and following him unless I was going to quit the job. But I had worked so hard to be where I was. So here I have this loving relationship that I really want and this wonderful career that I want, and I have to make that choice. I wanted to say to Gloria and the crew that said, you know, you're in a feminist movement; you can have everything. And I was like, no, you can't because there are some hard choices you have to make. I don't regret my choices. I believe that the Lord ordered my steps. I know I was at places and times where I helped people, whether it was in the courtroom or the community, whether it was as a result of my ability to let someone out of jail, put them on a special program, or expunge their record, I knew that I was there to encourage my daughter that you can have everything. Whitney, you can have a career and family because we built those bridges for you to cross. Had I not made that sacrifice and shown up every day in the workplace to be a valuable asset to the law firm, bench, community, or the US attorney's office, I'm not sure that my value would be seen in the same way, and perhaps those laws would not have passed. I'm still looking for the first female president of the United States. We're getting close.

Dr. Tucker: So, one last question. What advice do you have for the woman out there who needs to make a change, who needs to change how her life is going? What advice do you have for someone like that who's trying to make a change, either personally or professionally?

Judge Heard: First and foremost, to your own self, be true. I was a better mother. I believe it because I worked. The job I had was precious to me. It provided me an outlet for thinking and managing and impacting my community in a positive way, such that I came home with a feeling of pride and self-satisfaction in having done a good job that day. Not every person finds joy in working. Some people find joy in raising a family. That's what they do. That's what they do best. And that's their joy. Do it. Work from home if you can. What is it that makes you most happy? Because then you'll be a happy mother. You'll be a happy partner. You'll be a happy person.

Secondly, I believe in prayer. When all else fails, the Lord is on your side, who shall you fear? Who will you say, "I can't" to, when you have talked to the Lord and the Lord has heard you and has shown the way? I believe in prayer, I just do. I think that when all else fails, you get on your knees or straddle across the floor or however it works for you, and you ask the Lord for guidance and that's where the doors will open. The messages will be there for you, and they will send you in directions that you may not have expected or bring people into your life that will help you accomplish the goals that you have set for yourself. For others who really don't believe in a higher being, seek meditation. Get quiet with yourself. Think about what things bring you joy.

Those are the two things. Finally, always be willing to learn. Learn about yourself, learn about your world. We have computers now. Google a TED Talk. Just learn something; open a book. Find a way to learn something new. If you are a TV person, there is stuff other than HBO. Expand your mind.

Dr. Tucker: Yes. What better way to end things? So, thank you so much again for being here today and for granting me this opportunity to interview you. I know that others will be richly blessed by what you have shared.

Judge Heard: Well, I thank you. I hope my words help someone and they can use them in some way to encourage folks not to give up and to keep trying.

THANK YOU

Thank you for reading Reinvented to Rise Volume II

Please leave us a review by sending an email to info@joleaseenterprises.com with the Subject line Review Reinvented to Rise.

Do You Need Coaching Support

As a Reinvention Strategist, Alethia Tucker works with women 45 years plus, helping them to identify the purpose, passions and tools needed to create a personal and professional life that thrives. She can be contacted at atucker@joleaseenterprises.com. Visit www.joleaseenterprises.com, to access group and online programs.